LOCAL BOY

A Memoir

LEGACY ISLE
PUBLISHING

LOCAL BOY

A Memoir

FRED HEMMINGS

ISBN 978-1-935690-96-2
Library of Congress Control Number: 2017955893

Previously published material appearing in this book: "The Case for Professional Surfing" (*Surfer* magazine, 1966); "My Friend, Buffalo" (*Trim* magazine, 2014); "Thoughts While Jogging Through Campus" (Punahou School *Alumni Bulletin*, 1982); and "The Super Bowl with John Elway" (*The Honolulu Advertiser*, 1998)

Design and production
Jen Tadaki Catanzariti

Photos courtesy of Pan American World Airways (p. 18), Ron Haworth/State of Hawai'i Office of the Governor (p. 21), Leroy F. Grannis (p. 37), Kimo Wilder McVay (p. 57, p. 60 bottom), Pua Rochlen (p. 58 bottom), Dr. Don James (p. 63 top), White House Press Office (p. 66 top, p. 81), Twain Newhart (p. 66 bottom), Heath Hemmings (p. 69), Cline Mann (p. 54) and John S. Pritchett/*Honolulu Weekly* (p. 75). Additional photos from the Hemmings Collection.

Legacy Isle Publishing
1000 Bishop St., Ste. 806
Honolulu, HI 96813
Toll-free 1-866-900-BOOK
info@legacyislepublishing.net
www.legacyislepublishing.net

10 9 8 7 6 5 4 3 2 1

Printed in Korea

I wish to thank all who have enriched my life, including my many friends and, especially, my family, who have blessed me with their love and patience. *Mahalo*!

Contents

Preface

I **CANNOT THINK OF A BETTER PLACE** to have been born than Hawai'i and, better yet, growing up there in the second half of the twentieth century. What a wondrous era to be moving through time and space. In the relatively short years of my lifetime, humanity has leapt to the moon and the cosmos beyond. The wisdom of ages gone by has been recovered and nourished. Disease and other physical ailments are succumbing to the miracles of modern medicine. The mysteries of DNA, the body and the mind are now being comprehended. Humanity is approaching "singularity," in which computers can think and reason.

The years of my life defy my wildest dreams.

As I thought about writing this memoir, I couldn't make up my mind about the "personality" of the book. Would I write exactly what I think, or diplomatically avoid certain less-than-gentlemanly topics? Would I use civilized verbiage, or sink into the vulgarity that seems to permeate contemporary pop culture? It may be easier to to be vulgar, and to write whatever comes to mind. But maybe I should reach a little higher?

What should I include—everything from youth to the present day, everything I can remember and think would be of any interest to others? Or should I stay away from controversial subjects like politics and religion? Did your mom ever tell you not to talk about politics or religion at the dinner table? Mine did.

We'll see....

Introduction

I **CONSIDER MYSELF A BLESSED PERSON.**
I have a dynamic family with loving children and grandchildren.
Men and women of diverse backgrounds enrich my life.
I have lived in and loved Hawai'i since I drew my first breath.
From the crest of Mauna Kea, the cold of the snow goddess Poli'ahu
has chilled my soul.
My heart has pounded the rhythm of a chanting drum while running
across the blistering lava fields of Kona.
Upon the crest of Haleakalā, I have felt the golden rays of the dawn's
sun caress these Islands.
In the dark loneliness of Pāpalaua Valley on Moloka'i, I have heard
the wind whisper of ancient Hawai'i.
My back has ached from paddling countless strokes while racing a
koa canoe across the raging Kaiwi Channel.
In the shadow of Kōnāhuanui, I have felt the warriors' ghosts.
I have danced with the waves in the soft light of a full moon night in
Hanalei.
I have glided across the face of azure walls of water, while surfing the
mystical waves of Hawai'i.
All this is my wealth. I am a man of Hawai'i.

Aloha,

Fred Hemmings

Small Kid Times

1946

LILLIAN AND BIG FRED—MY PARENTS

L ILLIAN BERNICE FREITAS HEMMINGS My mother's family arrived in Hawai'i from Funchal, Madeira, Portugal, in 1883. She married Frederick Matthew Hemmings Sr., who was of English, Irish, French and Algonquin Indian descent. I was one of six half-Portuguese children. I have a lot of fun in my life being Portuguese.

Yes, the Portuguese jokes, if they have no ill intent, are often funny. The truth is that the Portuguese in Hawai'i have a noble and long history. Our history is rich. In the 1300s, Prince Henry of Portugal planted the seeds of world navigation and exploration. This was well before Columbus's famous journey across the Atlantic in 1492. The Portuguese soon became famous for navigating what was to be called the New World. Vasco da Gama, Magellan and other Portuguese men of the sea did indeed venture into the uncharted oceans of the world, bringing with them, for better or for worse, much of Western civilization.

Here in Hawai'i, the plantation era prompted the need for additional labor. The plantation owners soon set out to recruit contracted workers to make the long voyage to Hawai'i to work on the plantations on all the major islands. The first Chinese laborers came in 1852, followed by the Portuguese, mostly from the islands of Madeira and the Azores, beginning in 1877. Then the Japanese came in 1885, followed by Koreans and Filipinos at the turn of the twentieth century. Each ethnic group brought from its homeland a diversity of treasures, everything from ethnic customs and traits to a wide range of 'ono (delicious) food.

Hawai'i is unique in so many ways and one prominent way is that it's a state of ethnic minorities, in which no one group reigns supreme—unless you care to acknowledge that the Portuguese are truly God's chosen people. Just kidding!

The Portuguese are a tenacious and hardworking folk. Many were stonemasons and skilled laborers who helped build plantations and bustling towns. With the Portuguese came the Catholic religion. It appears that the Portuguese are indeed a matriarchal tribe. Portuguese men can be boisterous and outspoken, but at the end of the day the women rule the roost. So it is that the Portuguese are an intricate fiber in the tapestry of modern-day Hawai'i.

My mother, Lillian Freitas Hemmings, and me in 1948.

FREDERICK MATTHEW HEMMINGS SR.—"BIG FRED"

My mostly English-Irish father was a rough and ready character. He often reminded people he was also part (a very small part) Algonquin Indian and French. To his family he was a hardworking and hard-drinking Irishman. He arrived in Hawai'i in 1927 at the age of twelve. His father was a Navy man who was transferred to Pearl Harbor, where he worked in the fledgling field of Navy aviation. My father never left Hawai'i. He attended Lincoln School and transferred to Roosevelt for high school. Years later he liked to brag that he and a surfing buddy, Lex Brodie, planted the large banyan tree in front of the school.

As a young boy my father joined the Outrigger Canoe Club on then quiet Waikīkī Beach. He became a surfer and canoe paddler. He passed on his passion of paddling and surfing to all six of his children. He insisted that we all learn to steer canoes. We did. I steer Hawaiian outrigger canoes, as do my son and grandchildren. We are four generations of canoe steersmen and women.

1950

KĀHALA KIDS

I **HAVE FOND MEMORIES** of living at 4746 Farmers Road (curiously, I remember the address) in what eventually would become a plush neighborhood, Kāhala, from about 1950 to 1953. I was a small snot-nosed kid.

Farmers Road was named that because that's what it was—a road with farms. Bishop Estate, one of the largest property owners in the state, had not yet developed what is now residential Kāhala. Only Keala'olu, 'Aukai and Kāhala Avenues and a small portion of the crossroads were paved. Farmers was a dirt road. There were no paved roads between Farmers Road and lower Kaimukī. It was all farm lots.

My grandfather, Arthur Freitas, whom we knew as Uncle Arthur, leased a large farm lot with his and our house on it. He had horses. Just so you know, we called our handsome Portuguese grandfather "Uncle Arthur" because he was a bachelor and he most assuredly did not want us to call him "Grandfather" in front of his lady friends, who often were rather young. He was a dashing gentleman, and everyone knows that handsome Portuguese men are difficult for young ladies to resist!

Cynthia, my eldest sister, was the ruler of the clan, not because she was the eldest, but because she was the toughest. My brother, Mark, was the scholar. Maria was kind of a tomboy, but also was very pretty. My intrepid brother Aka was very independent. Heidi, the youngest, was somewhat blonde with bluish eyes. She pulled the English/Irish from my dad. Hence her nickname was "Irish." We all had nicknames. Mine was "Bully Beef." I never found out why.

Wai'alae Avenue was a two-lane road that weaved its way out to Kuapā Pond and Portlock in East O'ahu. It was the main thoroughfare from town. There was no Hawai'i Kai. Kuapā Pond was a large, isolated ancient Hawaiian fishpond. Lunalilo Home Road was mostly a dirt road leading to the Lunalilo Home for the aged. Many of the generous and kind *ali'i* of the Kingdom of Hawai'i bequeathed most of their land holdings in trusts to benefit the Hawaiian people.

At the corner of what is now Kīlauea and Wai'alae was a feed store named K. Okada. Across the street was an old *hongwanji*, which was turned into the first Star of the Sea Catholic school. I started kindergarten at the "old" Star of the Sea School. The school itself was housed in aging wooden structures and the church building appeared to be more of a barn than a church. Our teachers, the nuns, wore very modest habits with veils; only their hands and faces were exposed.

Most of the farm families in the neighborhood were Japanese. We had a gaggle of neighborhood kids to grow up with in the "country." Where Kāhala Mall now stands was nothing but an empty field overgrown with weeds. There was a bus depot kitty-corner from K. Okada store, with a shave ice stand where many local kids hung out at night.

We moved from 4746 Farmers Road when Bishop Estate decided to develop its acres of farm lots into the subdivision now called Kāhala. I bet you don't know what the theme was for the names of the streets of this new neighborhood that Bishop Estate built. These streets were named after Hawaiian birds, such as the *koloa* (native duck), *'elepaio* (flycatcher) and *pueo* (owl).

Good fun!

Playing in the banyan tree with my siblings, Butchie, Maria and Cynthia, ca. 1952.

1952

THE BANYAN TREE

I N OUR BACKYARD at 4746 Farmers Road was a huge banyan tree with limbs that reached out over the hard dirt ground. It was our playground. We played tag in the tree. One of the rules was that you couldn't touch the ground, so we became pretty good monkeys.

"Big Fred" warned us not to play tag in the tree because someone might fall from it. We were more afraid of the wrath of my father than of actually falling from the tree!

1954

THE POLIO EPIDEMIC

DR. JONAS SALK developed his anti-polio vaccination in the early 1950s. Polio prior to that was a major scourge and caused crippling and death for many around the world. This photo was taken in Dr. John Devereux's office on Punahou Street across from Central Union Church. The doctor's medical practice was in a little house that's still there, nestled between Shriners Hospital, now known as Shriners Hospitals for Children, and a high-rise. A local newspaper published this photo because four of us had had polio prior to the vaccine. My sisters Cynthia and Maria, older brother Mark and I all spent time in Kauikeolani Children's Hospital in Honolulu. (Years later Kauikeolani Children's Hospital merged with Kapiʻolani Hospital to form Kapiʻolani Medical Center.)

Wahiawa Photo Studio

ANTI-POLIO SHOTS — In their family physician's office, Mrs. Frederick Hemmings and her six children are inoculated with Salk anti-polio vaccine. Four years ago, before the vaccine was available, the four older Hemming children were in Children's hospital with polio. All have completely recovered, and the Hemmings are taking no chances. Dad got his later.

Fortunately none of us suffered any long-term effects.

It is important to note that almost all polio in the world has been eradicated by the Salk vaccine. The eradication of polio was accomplished through the generosity and kindness of members of Rotary clubs around the world. This reminds us that the true strength of any nation or culture can be found in the hearts of its people.

1954

KULI'OU'OU BEFORE KAISER

WHEN BISHOP ESTATE decided to develop Kāhala, it terminated our month-to-month farm lease. My grandfather, Uncle Arthur, and our family moved to a house on Kuli'ou'ou Road. Kuli'ou'ou Valley was dominated by the very large Reeves family. We all got along well because in part we all attended Holy Trinity Catholic Church together. A couple of the families in the valley were quite strong-willed. Some emerged as interesting characters in the years that followed. At the top of Kuli'ou'ou Road, about halfway up the valley, was a small store and dairy. The back half of the valley was a dairy farm, now long since gone.

We had great adventures exploring Kuli'ou'ou and Kuapā Pond. Neighborhood kids even made small canoes by bending a corrugated four-by-eight sheet of roofing material. We bent it in half lengthwise and hammered the two ends together against a piece of two-by-four wood to form a crudely shaped hull, and we sealed the ends with tar. It was a great adventure to explore the wilds of Kuapā Pond in our canoes.

Soon the East O'ahu community of Hawai'i Kai would be developed around the pond by famed industrialist Henry J. Kaiser and life would move on.

1964

LEARNING FOOTBALL AT PUNAHOU

SOME THOUGHTS from a Punahou football player of years gone by to players of years to be:

With the passage of time, the laurels of victory wither. Medals and trophies may tarnish and others will forget your years of playing football at Punahou School. As time must, the years will pass by—five, ten, twenty, soon forty, then fifty and, with blessings, more. With each year the treasure you have earned will become more glorious and gratifying. That treasure is your memories of the days of your youth on those Punahou teams. You will close your eyes and in your mind once again smell the sweat and turf of the field, and the sweet scent of the leis given to you at the end of the game. The roar of the crowd at the old Honolulu Stadium will be loud in your memory. You will experience and remember the tinny taste of your own blood. Some may recall vividly tearing tendons or having another player's spikes dig into your flesh, but it will no longer hurt.

As if it were yesterday, you will hear your father telling you to be strong—go to school, go to practice and don't let anyone know you're hurt. And you will remember the compassionate caress of your mother's hand, because she knew you were hurting. You will have learned to be strong through pain, and to be compassionate with others' pain.

In the years to come, you may meet those who shared those years with you. You may just meet an opponent who smacked you so hard that you didn't want to get up, and you will remember him offering you his hand to help you rise to your feet. You learned to play hard, but not to vanquish your opponent.

Someday you will be an aging man and you will run across an even older gentleman, whose years have made him frail, who was once a robust and invincible coach. You will reach out to your former coach and say two simple words, looking him in the eye with a firm handshake, "Thank you." You will have learned that life's treasures in so many ways are not necessarily any great achievements but, rather, the valiant efforts in the journey. Hopefully you are courageous, brave and true, for you are the Boys of Oʻahu.

Our Punahou football team played at the old Honolulu Stadium, aka the Termite Palace, at times before capacity crowds of 25,000 spectators. My number was 50. Here in 1962, my sophomore year, my classmate—and team leader—Charlie Wedemeyer is out in front of all his blockers, dancing down the field on one of his many long runs.

In uniform at Punahou's Alexander Field.

1965

PUNAHOU LXV

MEMORIES OF OUR YOUTH at Punahou become more valuable as each year passes. I recall my pals from football and those few who surfed. We were boys who played hard and had fun. In my view the class of 1965 had the most beautiful young ladies. They were all too smart to give me anything more than a passing glance. We were optimistic and eager to grow up. I now wished I had taken my time.

Our teachers cared for us as I am sure they do for students now. I did not study that hard. *Auwe*! All these years later I wish I could thank our teachers more, especially for their patience with me.

I remember the smell of leis mixed with sweat after football games, the excitement of winning and the "bummer" of a loss. Clear in my memory is Turkey Day 1964—the traditional Thanksgiving Day doubleheader—when Charlie Wedemeyer, Waynie Sterling, Stuart Wolfe, Bobby Klein and others led the Boys of Oʻahu to victory in the old Interscholastic League of Honolulu. More than 25,000 were packed into the "Termite Palace" to see Punahou reign victorious over the Kamehameha Warriors.

With fondness I remember all our coaches—Ralph Martinson, Dave Eldredge, Chubby Vicens and the indomitable Charley Ane. Coach Ane taught his boys some of life's toughest lessons that cannot be learned in a classroom—that is, how to win humbly and maybe more important, how to lose gracefully.

The truth is that surfing was a passion and not at the time a pervasive sport. After football season I went surfing. Sometimes football buddies would come along. One spring break a few of us went to Maui to surf a "secret" break called Honolua Bay. We surfed all day long with nobody else. It was magic.

The senior bench was one popular hangout, but I remember eating lunch really fast so that I could sit in the crux of the young monkeypod tree at the corner of Cooke Library. That tree's limbs now hang over the roof of the old library.

I most remember the treasured friends of LXV who have enriched my life greatly and have provided some of my most valuable treasures—memories of the days of my youth at Punahou.

Catch a Wave

1956

THE OUTRIGGER CANOE CLUB

MY DAD, AS A YOUNG BOY in about 1928, became a member of the Outrigger Canoe Club on Waikīkī Beach. He surfed and paddled. So despite our modest means, all of my family became members of the Outrigger Canoe Club. Well, my brothers and sister became enthralled with surfing and canoe paddling. We learned to steer canoes and that started a family tradition. On the beach at Waikīkī I grew up in the shadows of the great ocean men of Hawai'i, such as Duke Kahanamoku, John D. Kaupiko, George "Dad" Center and many more.

To this day the Outrigger is one of the world's most successful water sports clubs. Throughout the twentieth century the Outrigger was home to Olympic swimmers, divers and water polo players, world champion surfers and canoe racing teams led by the beloved Duke Kahanamoku. The Outrigger is even recognized as one on the founding arenas of beach volleyball. Through the years Outrigger volleyball teams have been international champions too. Outrigger athletes have brought Hawai'i and the nation many prestigious victories in water sports and volleyball, as well as Olympic medals.

The club was chartered in 1908 on the banks of Apuakēhau, which emptied the cool waters of Mānoa Valley into the Pacific. The founder of the club, Alexander Hume Ford, and the newly formed board of directors signed a long-term agreement to lease the land under the club from the Queen

Emma Estate. Hui Nalu Canoe Club was started at about the same time and was chartered in 1911.

Across the street from the club, in what is now the entrance to the International Market Place, was a parking lot. Back then, if you couldn't find a parking place on Kalākaua Avenue, you could park in this lot.

Our neighbors on the beach were the venerable Moana Hotel, built in 1901, and on the ʻEwa side of the Outrigger a small swimming club called Uluniu. Then there was the majestic Royal Hawaiian Hotel, which was built in 1927. During those years the travel market was dominated by Matson Navigation Company, which operated the *Lurline* and *Matsonia* steamships, among others. Pan American World Airways and United Airlines dominated the travel skies. Most visitors stayed at the Moana, the Royal Hawaiian Hotel or down the coast at the idyllic Halekūlani Hotel. Traveling to Hawaiʻi was a five-day odyssey on a steamship or an eight-hour-plus flight on a droning prop plane.

The original Outrigger Canoe Club was cleverly designed. The beach frontage was devoted to canoe sports and surfing. The second story of the clubhouse was for dining, and in the far corner of the property was the infamous Hau Terrace. I mention this because the new site of the Outrigger, down the beach across from Kapiʻolani Park, in my opinion is not well designed functionally. The beach frontage is mostly social, dining and drinking. Canoes and surfboards are kept near the street or even in the parking structure.

Late every afternoon the original beach boys and Outrigger Canoe Club regulars would enjoy adult beverages and good times on the Hau Terrace. Some would take naps under a *hau* tree near the Moana Hotel. I learned how to take a nap in the afternoon and often still do.

One of my life's great blessings was surfing as a youth in the company of the beach boys of the "romantic" era of Waikīkī. My friends included Steamboat, who took tourists out in the grand Ka Moi koa canoe. Panama Dave, Turkey, Dingo, Richard Wata, Koko and Harry were just a few of the colorful characters who made a living on the beach while having as much fun as possible.

The fifties were indeed romantic years on the beach at Waikīkī.

1958-2017

MĀKAHA IS THE BEST

SOMETIMES THERE ARE PLACES that communicate with you. You feel at home, as if that place is part of your essence. The surf at Mākaha makes me feel I belong there.

From "the Point," Mākaha sweeps into a gentle bay. The beach curves toward the Wai'anae Coast and a small rock point at the east end marks the boundary of Mākaha Beach. As with most bays, the deepest area is in the middle of the bay. During wet winters, rainwater from the valley would break through the beach and empty into the bay. That's probably why the coral is limited in the middle of Mākaha. On the point, the coral reef contours off the coastline, forming an ocean bottom that fashions the form and personality of Mākaha waves.

Mākaha is magic. I cannot think of any other surfing site where one morning you can surf gentle, fun, two- to four-foot waves and the next morning, twenty-five-foot-plus waves. That is Mākaha. There are tricks to riding big Mākaha. The waves have to be fifteen feet high or more to adequately break off the point.

At Waimea and other big wave spots you are challenged by dropping in on the takeoff and then you ride away from the peak of the impact zone. Though Waimea is a sensational takeoff and drop, Mākaha still is the ultimate challenge for paddling into and riding a big wave. This is because when you drop in at Waimea on a thirty-foot-plus day, you ride away from the impact zone. Riding big Mākaha takes more finesse; riding Waimea takes more courage. The modern-day pioneers of Waimea were "mountain men." Pat Curren and Buzzy Trent quickly became the poster boys of the original Waimea crew because of their bravado. All of the Waimea riders of the day are to be admired.

At Mākaha, when you drop into a huge wave, you have to ride across the bay about a quarter of a mile before trying to maneuver through the heavy impact zone known as the Mākaha Bowl. Riding big Mākaha takes much more skill. The aficionados at Mākaha catapult across the long wall, trimming high in the face of the wave. When you come to the Bowl, which sometimes is already pitching out, you fall down the face of the wave, gaining enough speed to sometimes go around the impact.

Waimea became sensationalized by pop culture surf media coverage. Mākaha is now the best-kept secret in big wave surfing.

Mākaha no kai oi!

At the Mākaha International Surfing Championships in 1966 with Hawai'i real estate developer Chinn Ho, Duke Kahanamoku and fellow big wave surfer Butch Van Artsdalen. My buddy, Jimmy McMahon, stands behind Chinn Ho.

ABC's *Wide World of Sports* host Jim McKay interviews me at the 1966 Mākaha International Surfing Championships.

1964

THE PERUVIAN INTERNATIONAL SURFING CHAMPIONSHIPS

I**N 1964, AT AGE SEVENTEEN,** during my junior year at Punahou, I flew from Honolulu to Peru on Pan American World Airways to compete in the Peruvian International Surfing Championships. Surfing on a Dick Brewer gun named "Baby Blue," I rode Peru's big wave site, the Kon Tiki break, and won the contest. The year 1964 was a good one—in the waves and on the football field.

Peru-bound with my carry-on item.

1966

THE CASE FOR PROFESSIONAL SURFING

I was an early advocate of professional surfing and in that capacity was asked to write the following article for Surfer *magazine in 1966.*

Surfing needs professionalism! The job a professional organization would do is to qualify surfing as a legitimate sport. Amazingly enough, though surfing is a part of life for more than a million people in the United States alone, it is not truly recognized as a sport. Surfing seems to be in a limbo—neither here nor there. Some claim riding waves is an art; others say it is a cult or a way of life. Still others say, no, surfing is a hobby or pastime that caters mostly to young people.

Surfing is not even recognized by the Amateur Athletic Union. The general public has yet to get a good explanation of what surfing really is, even though all the television networks have carried some type of surfing show for the past few years. Whether it be a big contest, special or included in a regular TV series (such as *Gidget*), surfing has not really been "qualified" as to what it really is.

Professionalism will make surfing legitimate. Once the naïve public, through the magic of television, sees a series of pro contests, it will be easy for them to realize that surfing is a clean, healthy S-P-O-R-T. Athletes winning money for their prowess and ability on all types of waves will clearly define the sport of surfing. Surfing then will be the most exciting and glamorous young sport in the world.

The effect that professionalism will have on competitive surfing will be for the betterment of all surfers. There are presently twenty to thirty top surfers in the world who are recognized as the surfing elite. Most hold this position because of their tremendous wave riding ability. They have spent many years and much concentrated effort to reach the top. They are in most cases financially capitalizing on their status.

1968

THE WORLD SURFING CHAMPIONSHIPS

THE 1968 WORLD CONTEST was a pivotal event in the history of surfing. First, it was the last major world championship with the best surfers competing as amateurs. Soon after, all the world's competitive surfing elite were involved in professional surfing. I retired from competitive surfing to work on developing pro surfing after the championships in Puerto Rico. I credit Eduardo Arena of Peru as the man who made it all happen. Peruvian surfers have become lifelong best friends. I try to visit them often.

Another interesting aspect was best described by a friend of mine, Barry Church, who called the '68 event an "Olympic event with a little bit of Woodstock." Surfing at the time was a Janus sport with two faces—one with the face of athletes and the other with a bevy of pop culture advocates, like far-out and righteous speaking surfers clad in Nehru jackets and flower power attire. I went to the awards banquet in a suit and was completely out of place. What's new?

The Territory of Puerto Rico and the government leaders very enthusiastically supported the event and it proved to be a wise investment. It seems that, as it is in Hawai'i, surfing was a huge promotional success for Puerto Rico. The contest ignited the surf and travel industry for the Rincon area. Years ago I noted that surfing is the main industry of the North Shore of O'ahu. So it is for Rincon, Puerto Rico. The short board revolution took hold at the event.

It was a pivotal contest. My mantra all these years has been and remains, "A few waves in Puerto Rico changed my life." So they did!

Presenting Governor John A. Burns of Hawai'i with the World Championship perpetual trophy for display at the State Capitol in 1968.

1968

SURFING—A JANUS SPORT

BY THE END OF THE SIXTIES surfing was a "Janus sport." That is, it had two faces. Some of us saw surfing as a healthy sport and surfers as clean-cut athletes.

Then there was the "pop culture" image of surfing in many ways being promulgated by a few self-ordained gurus, including many members of the surf media. The pop culture image of surfing being promoted was that surfing was more or less an antiestablishment sport. Along with it came an indulgence with drugs, especially LSD. Far out! There were a few surfers who became "heroes," not because of their surfing prowess, but more because they were "bad boys" who gave the finger to the dastardly "establishment." Interesting times!

I was an outspoken critic of drugs and "pop culture" as it was being promoted. I admit I was a zealot. It was a contentious issue then, and to this day still is. Sadly I saw talented young surfers lose or retard their lives because of drugs. I wrote an editorial that *Surfer* magazine published. Soon after, I retired from competitive surfing to own and operate pro surfing contests. The Pipe Masters is still going strong, and in 1976 Randy Rarick and I inaugurated the first world pro surfing tour.

To this day I still feel drugs and alcohol can be life-threatening addictions.

1969

THE WAVE MACHINE

IN LATE 1968 I successfully competed in the World Surfing Championships. As a result, in early 1969 I received a phone call from an executive with the Clairol/Bristol-Myers Corporation. He explained that they were developing the world's first man-made wave machine in, of all places, the desert in Tempe, Arizona.

They hired me as a surf consultant and I spent the summer of 1969 working on the project. The wave machine was at the end of a very large man-made pond that I helped design to accommodate the "machine swell" into a rideable wave. I sat in the pond and rode the first wave and many waves after that. It was a treat to be the only one surfing and riding the best waves—the only waves!—in Arizona. Even *Life* magazine covered the event.

Man-made waves are now being enjoyed around the world.

1976

THE FIRST SURF REPORT

IN THE EARLY SEVENTIES I received a phone call from Lawrence Berger, a downtown Honolulu businessman who owned KHVH "All News Radio." He asked me if I could do a surf report every morning on the radio. It would be the first surf report on radio ever, as far as he knew, so I signed on.

Looking back now, it was pretty archaic. Back then there was no high-tech satellite information. Nowadays, with all the precise data, surf prediction gurus can tell you within a foot how big the surf will be several days in advance.

During the summer we often received phone calls from friends in Tahiti saying a huge south swell was passing through. We learned less than three days later it would be big on the south shores of the Hawaiian Islands.

Because back in the early seventies there was little surf science and no internet, I did the next best thing; I called friends on the North Shore, in Mākaha and in Waikīkī and asked them how the surf was.

And that's the extent of what is thought to have been radio's first known surf report.

1977

INTERNATIONAL PROFESSIONAL SURFING

THIS IS THE LOGO of the first world tour organization, International Professional Surfing, the predecessor of the Association of Surfing Professionals and the World Surfing League.

I commissioned a Hawai'i-based artist to design the logo. The name is sometimes adulterated and called International Professional "Surfers" rather than "Surfing." In the early years I thought we needed cooperation between surfers and the event owners and producers and hence the generic name.

Randy Rarick and I started the world pro tour in early 1977 with the agreement of event organizers around the world. Patti Paniccia, a pioneer woman pro surfer, acted as the director of the women's world tour. Jack Shipley of Hawai'i was instrumental in refining a universal judging criterion. Big Bill Bolman of Australia, Peter Burness of South Africa and Kevin Sieter, director of the Malibu Pro event, were all most helpful.

The real heroes of the embryonic years of pro surfing were the athletes. Most surfers spent more money traveling around the world than they earned in competition. I believe that pro surfers are among the best athletes in the world because of their dexterity, flexibility and bravado. One week a pro surfer can be competing in fun six-foot surf in Biarritz, France, and the next week he can be plummeting down the face of a twenty-five-foot moving mountain of water at Waimea Bay in Hawai'i.

2012

THE SOUL OF SURFING IS HAWAIIAN

FOR THOUSANDS OF YEARS most cultures viewed the surf as one of nature's adversaries. But where many saw peril, the Hawaiians saw fun. From the alluring waves of Hawai'i was born the sport we now call surfing. The waves of Kalehuawehe (Castles) in Waikīkī, Mākaha and Paumalū (Sunset Beach) are the source of legends. We get a glimpse of the cradle of modern day surfing in old Waikīkī from the words of G. W. Bates, written in 1854:

> Within a mile of the crater's base (Lē'ahi, Diamond Head) is the old village of Waikīkī. It stands in the center of a handsome coconut grove ... there were no busy artisans wielding their implements of labor: no civilized vehicles bearing loads of commerce or any living occupant. Beneath the cool shade of some ever greens, or in a thatched house repose several canoes. Everything was so quiet as though it were the only village on earth, and the tenants its only denizens. A few natives were enjoying a promiscuous bath in the crystal clear stream that came directly from the mountains; some were steering their frail canoes seaward; others clad in nature's robes wading out on the reefs in search of fish.

It is hard to imagine that modern Waikīkī came from this idyllic setting. Waikīkī is now a vibrant and polished world destination.

The feat of surfing was viewed by the Western culture with astonishment. From the third expedition into the Pacific in 1778 by England came Captain James Cook's observation of surfing: "The boldness and address with which we saw them (Hawaiians) perform these difficult and dangerous maneuvers was altogether astonishing and scarce to be credited."

Hawai'i was thrust into a world exploding with change with the exposure to Western culture. The "Merrie Monarch," King David Kalākaua, did much to nourish and revive the ancient ways, including surfing and *hula*. Surfing suffered the impact of the rapid change and by the turn of the twentieth century the art of riding waves was almost lost. In 1908 on the banks of Āpuakēhau Stream on the beach at Waikīkī was founded the Outrigger Canoe Club and, soon after, Hui Nalu. To this day those two surfing and outrigger canoe clubs at Waikīkī are still the home of great watermen and women. From the waves of Waikīkī surfing survived into the twentieth century.

There is evidence that in 1885 three Hawaiian princes, David Kawānanakoa, Edward Keliʻiahonua and Jonah Kūhiō, made boards and surfed in Santa Cruz, California.

Though the princes surfed in California, the sport of surfing was not kindled there at the time. It was Waikīkī surfer George Freeth, a strikingly handsome Hawaiian, who is credited with introducing surfing to California. That's because after Freeth's appearance, surfing took hold in the waves of the Golden State. It is believed that Freeth was the "bronzed Mercury" made eternal by the words of novelist Jack London, who wrote:

> Where the moment before was the wide desolation and
> invincible roar is now a man, erect, full statured, not
> struggling frantically in that wild movement, not buried
> and crushed and buffeted by those mighty monsters,
> but standing above them all calm and superb, poised on the
> giddy summit, his feet buried in the churning foam, the
> salt smoke rising to his knees, and the rest of him in the
> free air flashing in the sunlight, and he is flying through
> the air, flying forward, flying as fast as the surge upon which
> he stands. He is a Mercury—a bronzed Mercury. His heels are
> winged, and in them is the swiftness of the sea.

The patriarch of modern day surfing is Hawaiʻi's beloved Duke Kahanamoku. Duke had a lifelong love affair with the ocean. The waves of Waikīkī were home to his heart. The waves of Waikīkī kept a smile on his face and a desire to share with aloha his heritage of surfing. In 1915 Duke rode the waves of Australia at Clearwater Beach. The Australians took to the surf with a passion. Duke also helped to popularize surfing on the East Coast of the United States. Those he taught to surf in Waikīkī often went home and took surfing with them to the shores of many lands. Duke Kahanamoku is honored in exotic surf sites such as Biarritz, France; Lima, Peru; and Australia, as well as in nearly every location in the world where people ride waves. Duke introduced surfing to the world with aloha and, for the first half of the twentieth century, surfing continued to grow slowly in popularity.

The Mākaha International Surfing Championships, inaugurated in 1954, became the first true world competition. Surfers from the major surfing locales traveled to Hawai'i every winter to compete in the waves of Mākaha. Often the surf would rise to twenty feet or more for the event. By the early 1960s the Mākaha contest was televised by the nationally broadcast program, ABC's *Wide World of Sports*. The Mākaha contest set the stage for modern-day international surf competitions.

Professional competitions soon followed and by the early 1970s events like the Pipeline Masters were recognized as surfing's premier contests. Expanding television coverage popularized surfing with people around the world. The world's first pro surfing circuit was conceived and inaugurated in Hawai'i in 1976. Professional surfing competitions are now held on the shores of the world's great oceans.

Early big wave riders from Hawai'i were extreme sports pioneers. They initiated the quest to ride the "biggest" wave. Tow-in surfing was spawned several decades ago on the island of Maui at a legendary site aptly named Jaws. It is difficult to believe that modern-day surfers are being towed by jet skis into ominous killer waves approaching 100 feet in height in locations such as Portugal and even many miles out to sea off the coast of California.

Hawai'i remains the ultimate testing ground for surfing. The fabled waves of the North Shore of O'ahu are the mecca in the world of wave riders.

The soul of surfing is Hawaiian. Surfing is Hawai'i's gift to the world.

Duke Kahanamoku and Friends

1965

THE MAN OF ALOHA

AS THE YEARS WANE ON, I now realize that one of the great blessings of my life was being a young surfer growing up in the shadow of Duke Kahanamoku.

There has been no one more beloved and respected in Hawai'i than Duke Kahanamoku. Why? It's an interesting question I've asked myself often. Duke was a man of great spiritual strength. That strength came from being a man of aloha. You could see the aloha in his eyes. Duke never spoke ill of others. Duke was kindhearted. Most of all, Duke wanted to share Hawai'i and the sport of surfing with everyone. He spent his life doing so and that is why I believe he is so revered.

There are many stories I could tell of my travels with Duke. One incident that best reflects Duke's creed of aloha happened at an event that well-known promoter Kimo Wilder McVay organized at the Waikīkī Shell. People from all over Hawai'i showed up to meet Duke. I was with him at the event when an older guy came up and said, "Duke Kahanawookawakawooka!" The gentleman could not even pronounce Duke's name properly. Some people might take their name being mispronounced as an insult, but not Duke. The old guy continued, "Duke, do you remember me? I met you when I was three years old." By now the guy was in his late forties, maybe early fifties, and I immediately said to myself, "How in the heck would anybody remember, forty-five or fifty years later, a three-year-old kid he met somewhere?"

Duke looked the man in the eyes and with a smile said, "Nice to see you again." That was Duke Kahanamoku. The old guy's face lit up like he'd just received a great gift, which he had. The man had wanted to be recognized and Duke had recognized him. Although I surmise that he did not remember a three-year-old boy he'd met years before, Duke gave him the gift of recognition. That was the character of Duke Kahanamoku. That's how he treated everybody.

Duke never measured people by the content of their pocketbook; he measured them by the content of their character. Therefore, like the beach boys of old, Duke was friends with everybody. You could be the janitor at the Royal Hawaiian Hotel and Duke would sit there and talk with you and enjoy your company just as much as he enjoyed the company of a political leader or movie stars like Bing Crosby or Shirley Temple. Duke was everybody's friend, with aloha.

As time went on and I spent more time with Duke, I learned there was much more to surfing than just riding waves. Surfing is a lifestyle that should be shared and respected. It grieves me so much that nowadays some "locals" use being from Hawai'i, or being part Hawaiian, as an excuse to claim stewardship, or ownership, of the waves and of Hawai'i. Duke knew that the waves were a gift for everyone to enjoy.

Duke was a renowned swimmer who won Olympic gold medals, as well as a champion outrigger canoe steersman and paddler, and Hawai'i's ambassador of surfing. He took surfing to the shores of Australia and to other places in the world. Duke was also a very clever wave rider.

Sit Outside and Wait for the Best Wave

Duke imparted knowledge that served me well in my years of riding waves, especially in a certain 1968 contest in Puerto Rico. I learned a very interesting lesson from Duke's legendary ride in 1917. Before I share it with you, let me first ask a question. Is it better to ride many good waves or is it better to wait outside, be patient and wait for the best wave? This is a question with no right or wrong answer. You can ride any wave you want, any way you want.

By the turn of the millennium, my desire to ride really big waves had waned. A fifteen-foot day at Mākaha was about as big as I wanted to surf. I learned to watch the weather reports very closely. Whenever the waves on Oʻahu's North Shore were huge, the place for me to be was Mākaha. I confess that I wanted to catch the backside of big swells so that I was not in the lineup when the waves increased to a size I no longer was comfortable being in. Fear has a threshold, and mine was considerably less than when I was younger and surfing with reckless abandon. I knew I still could handle fifteen-foot waves at Mākaha.

Mākaha is special and I know her well. I know where the sweet spot is to take off. I know how to ride the wave high so you gain enough falling speed to make it through the bowl before it explodes. The waves don't come straight in at Mākaha. Rather, they bend around Kaʻena Point. Sitting on the point at Mākaha on a big day, you can see the swell relentlessly marching down the coast.

Once, after figuring out that the swell would peak in the middle of the night, I decided to make a sunrise journey to Mākaha. At dawn's early light I arrived. The waves that morning were fifteen feet and perfect! The crowd was sparse. In fact, there was no crowd.

Shortly after I paddled into the lineup, a large set appeared off in the distance. As I watched the set march down the coastline, my heart began to beat faster. I paddled to where the best takeoff spot would be and stroked into the peak wave of the set. Years before I had learned to count the waves in a set and sense the rhythm of the day. On the big days at Mākaha it's about fifty-fifty whether you will make the wave. Stroking into a Mākaha wave, unlike on Oʻahu's North Shore, was easier. I trimmed high and flashed across the fast moving wall of water and blew out the end of the wave as the bowl collapsed behind me. Wow! Such an incredible rush! I sat in the channel and said to myself, "It's not going to get any better than that." So I paddled to the inside, caught some whitewater to shore and then drove back into town.

Some people might find it odd that I had driven from town to Mākaha, paddled out at dawn and rode just one wave. Yet that's the lesson I learned from Duke Kahanamoku. One great wave is better than many good waves. I still remember that wave I rode in 2000.

Thanks, Duke.

Good times with Duke Kahanamoku on the beach at Waikīkī.

ca. 1967

DORIS DUKE

I **WAS A YOUNG MAN** just out of high school when I received a phone call from a Portuguese gentleman. He was the house manager of famed heiress Doris Duke at Shangri La, her Moroccan flavored home on the Waikīkī side of Black Point. The home could better be described as a Moroccan art palace. Doris Duke was at the time known as the world's wealthiest woman.

I was very fascinated that the much older Doris Duke would want to have dinner with a young surfer from Hawai'i. I went.

We sat at a modest sized table on her patio, not in the grand formal dining room. Dinner was served with a Rothschild wine, which was most enjoyed. Of course everything was elegant. She spent the evening asking questions and talking about the Kahanamoku brothers, beach boys and surfers of Waikīkī from years gone by. My curiosity as to why she wished to have a young surfer over for dinner was answered in part. I guess she missed the carefree days of her youth and of frolicking with the band of merry men of the beach at Waikīkī.

I found out later that Doris Duke had had a torrid love affair with Sam Kahanamoku, one of Duke's brothers. She, like so many celebrities, movie stars and wealthy visitors of the era, had a fascination with this legendary band of brothers of Waikīkī Beach. No doubt this was partly due to the fact that when she was with them, she was treated like one of the gang, not like the richest lady in the world.

Our dinner was quite pleasant. I hope I rekindled pleasant thoughts and warm memories of her years as a young *bon vivant* in the Hawai'i of yesteryear.

2014

MY FRIEND BUFFALO

My friend Richard "Buffalo" Keaulana is a man with many faces. Buffalo is a modern day aliʻi who leads not by force but by example. He is a consummate waterman and has passed his legacy on to his children. He is a devoted husband to a beautiful and strong woman, Momi. Buffalo is a surfing ambassador. Buffalo is wise. Buffalo also has a clever sense of humor that has kept us both laughing a lifetime.

To know Mākaha is to know Buffalo. Back in the late 1940s and early fifties, the North Shore of Oʻahu wasn't the prime destination for big surf. In those days, Mākaha was the place where town surfers would go to ride big waves.

By the late fifties, as a young boy, I remember first venturing to the Mākaha International Surfing Championships, a true carnival of surfing events. At that time, the Mākaha contest was *the* contest. The winner at the Mākaha event was the de facto world champion. As a young boy I watched a rugged-looking Hawaiian called "Buffalo" riding the waves. He body-surfed, he board surfed and he rode the big point waves when they were breaking. Buffalo was also a superb spear fisherman and diver. Buffalo owned Mākaha.

In 1965 Hawaiʻi's surfing leaders, led by the respected Wally Froiseth, selected a team to go to the inaugural World Surfing Championships in Peru. Buffalo and I were teammates. We shared a room in Lima in an old hotel named Leuror, in a sleepy coastal neighborhood named Miraflores. The contest was held in large surf in Punta Rocas, a point surf on the edge of Punta Hermosa Bay, down the coast from Lima. Punta Rocas is a large peak that forms into a hot right slide, much like Sunset Beach on Oʻahu. There are long gentler lefts that peel into the bay.

In the competition, Buffalo caught this one very large wave and rode the left slide all the way around the side of the point into the bay where the judges couldn't even see him. Laughingly, I later asked him, "Eh, how come you rode all the way into the bay? The judges couldn't see you." Buffalo's response: "It was a good wave." That simple answer explained his priorities perfectly.

Buffalo and I were both fascinated by the Peruvian culture. We visited museums and attended a formal reception at the presidential palace. The Peruvians are a gregarious and hospitable people. Most Peruvian surfers at the time were members of Club Waikīkī, which was founded in 1941 by the venerable Carlos Dogny, a surfing pioneer, renowned gentleman and bon vivant.

On the short walk from Club Waikīkī back to our hotel, vendors sold fruits and vegetables from carts on the side of the road. One cart offered big juicy looking watermelons. The dollar was very strong, and for very few sols, the Peruvian currency, we bought the whole cartful. We had the fellow selling the watermelons bring them to our little hotel, where we put all of them in the bathtub. After drinking some beer, we cut the watermelons in half and had one of the greatest watermelon fights *ever*. Afterwards, it looked like our room had been the scene of some sort of bazaar Incan human sacrifice. It took quite a long time to clean up the room, but luckily we had some help.

Buffalo is not a formally educated man in the book sense, but he's certainly one of the wisest men I know. Years ago, in the late sixties, some surfers got caught up in LSD. "Acid" was a strong and unpredictable hallucinogenic drug that quickly led to an epidemic of sorts. A handful of surfers were more or less LSD gurus. In some ways the LSD cult was quite humorous, though sadly, the drug destroyed lives. The LSD aficionados had their own way of talking and dressing. I often joked that they were like a Cheech and Chong convention. On the other hand, Buffalo had a sense of reality in which drugs had no place.

One day after surfing, we were sitting around drinking beer, which we used to do *very* well, and this one character whose name I won't mention was talking about the "magic" of LSD, how it opens up your mind and how you can see beyond the reality of reality—pure gibberish, but sounding very highfalutin. This surfer said that reality is only what you perceive it to be and that we could, for instance, only be imagining that we were sitting there on the beach drinking beer and talking.

Buffalo had had enough of that. He looked at the guy and said, "Hey, how 'bout I slap your head? Are you gonna imagine that?" Of course, that jolted the conversation back to reality, and our guru friend got the hint about an imminent "reality" that might be bestowed upon him. Buffalo has a way of expressing common sense that is easily understood; there's no equivocating.

Hunting in the Sixties

For a couple of years in the late sixties, we got on a hunting kick. Buffalo decided that we'd all go rat hunting. And I asked, "What—what do you mean, Buffalo?" He said, "We're gonna go rat hunting." I had a crazy friend who was a gun collector, so I headed out to Mākaha with my friend in his car. When we got to the west side, my friend threw open the trunk of his car and showed us what appeared to be a full-on arsenal. I'm sure we'd be thrown in jail today for the number of guns he had in that trunk. So we loaded up a few shotguns and .22 rifles and went into remote Mākua Valley.

I'm sure not many of you are rat hunters, but basically rats sleep in tree nests during the day. So we would shoot the nests with .22s and the rats would come running out. Then we dispatched them efficiently with the shotguns.

After a few hours of big game rat hunting we heard sirens blaring and we wondered, "What the heck's going on?" Pretty soon cops came racing up, jumped out of their cars and said, "What the hell are you guys doing? Buffalo! What are you doing with those guns?" The cops seemed partially upset and I think amused. They informed us that we couldn't be shooting rats on even remote public beaches no matter how much of a public service we thought it was. That was the end of our rat hunting career, but that wasn't the last time I went hunting with Buffalo.

Sitting at Buffalo's house on the beach at Mākaha one day when there were no waves, we decided to go turkey hunting. Buffalo lived on the beach because he was the lifeguard and a beach attendant there. Right across the street from Buffalo's house were wild turkeys in a section of Mākaha Valley owned by real estate developer Chinn Ho. Buffalo and I walked across the street and, being the big game hunters we thought we were, meandered our way *mauka*. About halfway up an old dirt road, we spotted a turkey, which we managed to shoot from a good distance. We were in the bushes, about a mile up the valley, and Buffalo said, "I'll carry it for now." He threw it over his shoulders and carried it down the road. We were still hidden by the bushes and nobody could see that we had shot one of Chinn Ho's turkeys.

But when we approached the edge of the kiawe growth right before the public road, about to walk in full view with our bagged turkey, Buffalo threw it on the ground and said, "Now, Freddie, it's your turn to carry it." That's how clever Buffalo is. If anyone was going to get busted, it would be me!

Later, Momi cooked the turkey. We didn't eat it; it was so tough we couldn't even bite into its flesh. To this day I call it the BF Goodrich turkey because it was like trying to chew a rubber tire.

There are many more Buffalo adventures and memories that are part of my life's treasures. Together Buffalo and I have experienced many blessings, challenges and laughs. I am lucky to call Richard "Buffalo" Keaulana my friend.

Hanging with Chubby Mitchell (left) and Buffalo in Mākaha. With his stutter and great wit, Chubby was one of the finest men I ever knew. "Freddie," he would say, "if can, can. If no can, no can." He was right!

In the early sixties, Buffalo Keaulana and I were featured in a print ad promoting colorful Jams swimwear.

2014

UNDER THE HAU TREE

I HAVE A PICTURE OF MY DAD paddling a racing canoe in 1934. My father loved to surf and paddle, and he passed his love of the ocean in turn to each of his six children. My dad grew up on the beach at Waikīkī, so it was natural that this was also my own playground as a young boy. As far back as I can remember I didn't go to parks to play. Instead I went to the beach. My sports were surfing and canoe paddling. So it is for my children and my children's children.

Being a young boy in the fifties and early sixties, I was fortunate to grow up in the shadow of Duke Kahanamoku and the surfers and legendary beach boys of Waikīkī. These men were the greatest surfers of the day, and most of them called the Outrigger Canoe Club, Hui Nalu and Waikīkī Surf Club home. I never was introduced to any of the beach boys; I just grew up knowing them. One of the people who came to the Outrigger to surf was Duke Kahanamoku.

I got to know Duke at a young age. I'd say, "Hi, Duke," and he'd say, "Hi, boy." Duke called many others "boy" too. For Duke, it was a term of endearment. In fact, until he passed away Duke continued to call me that. "Hey, boy, where you going?" It really was heartwarming when I look back on it now.

When I was a kid, Duke would invite others along when he was about to paddle out. "Hey, we're going surfing," or "Hey, let's go catch some waves." Duke's peers, surfers like Reverend Abraham Akaka, John D. Kaupiko, Lorrin Thurston, Fred Steere and Art Schofield, would join him. There weren't many small squirt kids surfing. But I was a small quirt kid, and I would often find myself sitting on the inside with a few others, or sometimes alone with some of these great men of Hawai'i sitting outside.

There was a very definite protocol. You would sit on the inside to take off on a small wave, but you never would take off on a wave in front of them. The old-timers on their battleship boards would run you over. Those were the unwritten rules and you respected them. You minded your place in the lineup. You knew to wait for your turn. The day would come when a young wave rider could join the surfers riding the waves on the outside, waiting for the bigger sets. In the meantime, you did not get in the way. We respected these men as gentlemen.

There was an untold, unacknowledged spirit in surfing. Those men—and women too—loved the sport so much that they wanted to share it. They would say, "Ah, come on—let's go surfing," or "Come on, boy, let's go catch some waves." Aloha and sharing was part of the spirit of riding waves. How lucky I was to grow up in the chivalrous era of surfing. Certainly Duke and his pals had been the best in the early twentieth century. As a young boy, I respected Duke, but I didn't know him as a luminary. He was, obviously, someone very special. He was Duke. He didn't act like someone who needed adulation.

Thoughts of Duke bring to mind the Outrigger Canoe Club. The original Outrigger Canoe Club was right on the beachfront between the Royal Hawaiian Hotel and the Moana Surfrider Hotel. In front of the club, sitting on the beach, were all of the club's koa outrigger canoes. At the corner of the club there was a bank of lockers right next to the exit to the beach. My locker was in the back, furthest from the ocean. The bank of lockers housed the most incredible cross section of surfboards. It was a view of the history of surfing. Those lockers held old skegless wooden boards from the 1920s, and hollow boards designed and built by famed waterman Tom Blake in the thirties. There were modern South American balsa boards. Many of the old hardwood boards didn't have the newfangled covering called fiberglass. It was an absolute treasure trove of surfboards.

While Hui Nalu did not have a clubhouse, that club's members would hang out under a hau tree right next to the Outrigger. There was a large area between the hau tree and the Moana. A few Hui Nalu koa canoes sat majestically on the beach there, as koa canoes had for more than 1,000 years.

Some of the beach boys and surfers would take naps in the late afternoon, in the cool shade of the comforting hau tree. Seeing all of these guys lying down and sleeping under the hau tree was contagious. I quickly picked up the habit and observe it to this day. When I was a Hawai'i state senator at the State Capitol, I often would ask the staff to close the door and intercept phone calls for a half hour while I napped. It wasn't quite like lying on the beach at Waikīkī under the hau tree, feeling the caress of soft trades, but the nap still made things good. I am grateful to Duke and the beach boys for teaching me that valuable lesson. Try it!

Those men lived a very romantic lifestyle. I believe that part of Duke's aura was this lifestyle of intrinsically knowing what is important in life and what is not. Unfortunately, some people nowadays think that the things you can buy with money are what's important. Duke and many of his friends understood that it isn't money or possessions but rather enjoying the simple things—like the fellowship of surfing with friends—that are life's greatest riches.

Old-timers at left-slide Canoe's in Waikīkī. As a kid, I learned not to get in the way of these guys—they'd run you right over!

Run, Freddie, Run!

1970s

THE JAMES WALKER AUSTIN INVITATIONAL MARATHON

I**T WAS IN THE LATE SEVENTIES.** Best buddies Kimo Austin, Bruce Ames and I were sitting around shooting the breeze following an afternoon jog. Our conversation meandered around several profound subjects, like how big would the waves be tomorrow and other important issues of the day. We got to talking about marathon running. All of us had run a few. I was feeling pretty good—in top shape, as the saying goes. Then I made the terrible mistake of betting that I could run a three-hour-and-thirty-minute marathon. My previous best was about three hours and forty-two minutes, so a twelve-minute leap in time would be about one-half minute per mile faster. It doesn't seem like much, but if you know marathons, it is. At the time, there was a tribe of people at the Outrigger Canoe Club who ran almost every day. The usual course went from the club to the service station at the top of Kealaʻolu Avenue in Kāhala and back. It was eight miles round-trip.

The Honolulu Marathon Association put white lines on the route every mile from the start of the marathon to the finish. Because running can be mind-numbing, I would keep track of my time with my very expensive Casio running watch (I think it cost me $13 and it worked like a champ). But back to my ill-conceived statement, "I bet I could run a three-and-a-half-hour marathon." Kimo immediately jumped on the opportunity and said, "I will take that bet." At this point, testosterone overrode common sense and I said,

"Alright, you're on." Bruce Ames jumped in and said, "Me too." Bruce then said, "I bet a case of Heineken beer." Bruce often said that Green Devil Heineken beer was the elixir of life. I think he learned that from my dad; Bruce was like another son to him. Kimo and I discussed what we would bet. We finally came up with dinner for two at the very upscale Canlis in Waikīkī, one of Honolulu's premier restaurants.

Sensing that I had made a mistake with the bet, I tried to buy some time and suggested that we hold the race a month later. My dear friend Kimo immediately shot back, "Oh no, next Sunday." Ouch. That gave me almost no time to prepare. So early Sunday morning Kimo picked me up. I brought along some containers of water. Kimo was going to be the race official and was going to maintain the aid stations, as well.

The next thing I knew, I was standing alone in the dark on Nimitz Highway downtown, a few minutes before 6 a.m. This was the official starting line of the Honolulu Marathon. Kimo asked if I was ready because we were going to begin at exactly 6 a.m. To spoof Kimo, I got down in a sprinter's stance like I was leaving the blocks on a 100-yard dash.

The race began with the fanfare of Kimo's voice, "Ready, set, go!" I ran enough to know that a big mistake in marathon running was to blow out too fast and then crash at the end. I knew I had to keep a pace of eight minutes a mile or a little less to break three and a half hours. It was a long Sunday morning run out to Hawai'i Kai. Every five miles or so, Kimo dutifully handed me water as I ran briskly by him. At the back of Hawai'i Kai, my bearded barrister friend, Bruce Stopford Ames, drove up next to me to check on his wager. He had the pained look of a man realizing I was on pace to win the big bet. He started asking me questions and talking to distract me, to wear me down with idle chatter. I told him in a most gentlemanly manner to, "Shut the f--- up." He laughed. And so it went as I headed back down Kalaniana'ole Highway, carefully monitoring my expensive Casio watch.

I turned the corner on Keala'olu Avenue, which left me about four miles to the finish. It was then that I hit the legendary "runner's wall." That's when your body tells you in very explicit terms, "Stop running, stupid." I couldn't stop; I was too close to give up. Fortunately for me, another dear friend and a man of great athletic prowess, John Finney, who had run out to meet me, began escorting me to the finish line. John was great with words of encouragement.

There's a slight grade from Black Point Road to the crest of Diamond Head Road. For exhausted people running the Honolulu Marathon, it is like climbing Everest. Every step was painful. I knew that once I reached the crest, running downhill would be my reprieve. Unfortunately, I was so depleted that I switched into automatic pilot as my brain gave up on common sense. I do remember, vaguely, getting on the sidewalk at Kapi'olani Park for the half mile or so to the finish.

Coming up the sidewalk in the other direction was a gaggle of Sunday morning joggers. John and I knew that I was very close to achieving the 3:30 goal. He yelled ahead, "Clear the sidewalk, runner! Clear the sidewalk!" I was running like a truck with no brakes. All the joggers in the pack wisely got off the sidewalk except for one guy; he wasn't going to cooperate. I kept running and had to move to the side a bit in order not to hit him head on. Unfortunately for him, he got winged by my right forearm that hit him in the chest. I could hear him yelling four-letter curse words. When I crossed the finish line, Kimo and I pressed the stop buttons on our watches. Both had me within a second or two of 3:31:22. I had lost.

The case of Heineken was delivered to Bruce Ames, and he consumed it with much gusto.

A week later, Kimo and I were at Canlis on Kalākaua Avenue. this elegant restaurant was housed in an award-winning architectural structure and was considered a premier watering hole for Honolulu's blue bloods. Karl, the *maître d'*, escorted us to one of the best tables. On the mauka side of the venerable restaurant tall, opened vents allowed the cool trade winds from Mānoa Valley to filter through the establishment. We enjoyed a superb dinner with a lot of laughs. After dessert I realized that besides running the world's dumbest marathon, I would have to pay a hefty dinner tab for doing so—a double whammy.

I asked the *kimono*-clad waitress for the check. She politely told me Mr. Austin already had taken care of the bill.

1982

THOUGHTS WHILE JOGGING THROUGH CAMPUS

WHILE LIVING IN MĀNOA VALLEY, I often went on evening jogs. One evening my long jog took me to Punahou. Feeling good, I decided to run through the campus on my way back up the valley to home. I ran in the front gate and took a route through the Academy buildings. The minute I rounded McNeil Hall, "my tree" came to mind.

Is it strange, Tree, that after all these years I gravitated to you? It does seem like only yesterday that I used to lean against you during breaks and sit on your young limbs during lunch period. The campus has changed—new buildings, roads, ways to come and go—and you have changed, too. Curiously, I notice the change in you so much. You are so very big; when I spent my time with you, you were barely as tall as Cooke Library. Now, I can see that they trim your branches so they won't hang over the roof.

Hey, remember the guys who used to hang around you? I always raced through lunch so I could get to you first and sit up on your branches. Remember Dougie and Dale? They're still around. I think Dougie is on Kaua'i. Dale is in Kona. Clifford is there too! Old Frankie Cook. He's doing well, happily married the last I heard. And Charlie. God keep him and his loved ones. I think Wayne Sterling is still in Tahiti. He's got kids there. And Bobby Klein is a judge. Isn't that great? Wolfe and McAndrews are around. I saw Kneubuhl a few years back at the Alumni Lū'au.

We aren't carefree kids anymore. You remember the silly things we talked about and all the fun we had as we hung around wasting time. Time has made its mark. You, Tree, are somehow so enduring. Standing under your branches transports me back to those years. For the few moments I am alone with you, I feel so overwhelmed with memories. I guess life moves from episode to episode, and memories are the best things to take along that no one can steal. Hey, Tree, I'm rested. I'm going to go home now. Boy, it's been great! Oh yeah! My kids are here at school. My boy's in sixth grade. My little girl just started kindergarten. I wonder if they will get to know you. I sure enjoyed those years. Thanks for reminding me.

See you later, Tree.

1994

RUNNING

I **HAVE ENJOYED NUMEROUS SPORTS** my entire life, including running. I'm not built for running, but no one told me that! I have run marathons and other races, and I've already described my one lonely and, I might add, not-so-smart marathon. Running became more than just a competitive sport. I most enjoyed solitary runs in the mountains, sometimes running by myself at night on full-moonlit mountain trails and sometimes on the beaches at low tide. For a number of years I ran with an equally crazed night runner named Kent Bein. Usually for a night run we would start at 10 p.m. and run on mountain trails to well past midnight.

One of the most beautiful moments ever was when Kent and I were running the Maunawili Trail to Waimānalo on a cool full-moon night. About halfway to Waimānalo we rounded a Koʻolau ridge that was a high promontory. It was very still and eerily quiet; the luminescent moon was bright, casting a blue hue over the Windward Coast. It was ethereal. We stopped running and pulled plastic ponchos from our butt packs to lie next to the trail and bask in the soft light of that eerie night. Surely God was on the altar high on that Koʻolau ridge. He touched us.

Sadly, Kent died young. I miss him, but treasured memories of our runs bring a smile and joy. Around the year 2002, my arthritic hip finally required a hip replacement, which brought my running career to a screeching halt. Running was a good addiction that I miss very much.

Unfortunately, a family history of arthritis on my mother's side, combined with physical abuse of my own body, resulted in numerous orthopedic problems, including several operations on each knee and the eventual replacement of my left knee and right hip with titanium joints. The doctors tell me that my right knee and left shoulder socket now need to be replaced too.

I often joke that I have to change my will. It was my original intent to be cremated and have my ashes taken to join Duke and my friends beyond the reef. However, due to an overabundance of titanium joints, I will have to be melted down.

1996

HALEAKALĀ

MY LIFELONG BEST FRIEND, PAT BOWLEN, and I vigorously pursued "adventures" in Hawai'i. Over the years we have run to Keanakolu Cabin on Mana Road, at the 6,000-foot elevation on the slopes of Mauna Kea. Together we have paddled on the lonely and remote north coast of Moloka'i, where we slept overnight in sprawling Wailau Valley. (On that occasion, Pat and I, along with several others, were the valley's only habitants.) We have run in the blistering heat on the King's Trail traversing the lava fields of the Kona Coast. Due to our competitive natures, all of our runs were more or less races.

But our most arduous and rewarding adventure was running through the majestic Maui volcano, Haleakalā, the House of the Sun. We arrived at the 10,023-foot summit before sunrise. Seeing dawn's warm early light creep over the Islands reminded us that there is a God. The plan was to run through the crater and exit into the parking lot at an elevation of 8,000 feet, where our wives, Annabelle and Suzy, would pick us up. Pat and I were not overly equipped for what would be a "death run." We had small water bottles in our butt packs and a few chocolate bars. The faulty logic was that once we started running we would be warm enough not to need jackets. We ran in jogging shorts and long-sleeved tee shirts. At the start of our run, the temperature must have been in the high thirties.

The journey down Sliding Sands Trail was a run of long, loping strides. We met a throng of well-equipped campers walking out of the crater. They watched us run by, convinced that we were "not all there." They were correct.

What a joyous, albeit cold, run to the floor of the crater! We didn't even notice the thin oxygen of the high altitude. At an intersection at the bottom of Sliding Sands is a tree offering a pleasant place to relax. We "relaxed" for what must have been twenty-seven seconds. The journey across the floor of the crater is, I imagine, like running on Mars. It is a feast for the senses. The middle of the crater is one of the quietest places on Earth. Cinder cones born from ancient times rise up from the ashes of the floor of the crater. They are Martian red. On a trail, it is not easy to run up and down the soft sides of the cinder cones. We drank our meager rations of water. Beyond the cinder cones was a winding path through an *aʻa* lava field. The lava is crunchy and jagged. Because of the rugged terrain, each step has to be taken with caution.

We finally arrived at Hōlua Cabin. The National Park Service maintains several cabins for overnighters. They are always booked. At the cabins there is a catchment water tank. We sucked at the faucet like nursing babies.

Several overnighters from the cabins emerged and one young lady looked at Pat and inquired, "Aren't you Pat Bowlen?" She went to school in Colorado, where most know and recognize the owner of the Denver Broncos. We got the same look from them, as in, "We can't believe you're both dumb enough to run through this crater."

Before us was the biggest test. The crater floor at Hōlua Cabin must be at an elevation of about 6,000 feet. The parking lot where we would exit was at about 8,000 feet. Two thousand feet doesn't sound like too much. Wrong! The first half of the run back out of the crater is a switchback trail etched into the face of the cliff in the 1930s by Franklin D. Roosevelt's Civilian Conservation Corps.

We would not admit that we were totally exhausted. Hauling my stout body up 2,000 feet was severe. About halfway up the cliff we ran through a cloud. We were depleted and desperately needed water. There were puddles on the trail. Pat and I dropped to our knees like thirsty dogs and sucked the icy water from the top of the puddles.

Near the top we ran around the edge of the rim so that we emerged on the outside of the crater. Off in the distance was the parking lot. It was a matter of macho honor to get there first. Pat won—this time.

Years later I marched through the crater again with a very special family, the Buetners. After a cold night in a tent at Hōlua Cabin, I succumbed to an atrial fibrillation attack. My dear friend Austin Buetner convinced a pack horse escort to pack me out, too. My two young grandsons, Trevor and Merrick, who were with me, hiked out with the Buetners.

Years ago I had raced through the crater on foot with Pat. Now I was being packed out on horseback.

Yikes! I tried to hide at the summit to avoid further humiliation.

Hoe Wa'a: Outrigger Canoe Racing and Surfing

1964

CANOE SURFING

CANOE SURFING DATES BACK to ancient Hawai'i. By the 1950s, the only surfing in outrigger canoes was being done with tourists in Waikīkī at, appropriately, the Canoe's break fronting the Moana Hotel.

In 1964 the Outrigger Canoe Club moved to its new location at the foot of Diamond Head. We took our canoes with us, including the large surfing canoe. Soon we were riding waves at the surf break called Old Man's, on the edge of the Kapua Channel fronting the club. During the summer, large swells generated by storms as far away as New Zealand often resulted in "first break waves" in Waikīkī. "First break" meant really big. We would take the surf canoe out to Castle's, as Old Man's would close out.

Soon after, a four-man surfing canoe went into production. Unlike the bigger tourist canoes, the four-man canoes were very maneuverable. Naturally, being testosterone-driven surfers, we tried to ride the biggest waves possible. By the late sixties we were riding Big Castle's in canoes. Wipeouts were brutal. One of the foolish unwritten rules of the game was not to jump out of the canoe when peril loomed. However, peril often ruled and we bailed out.

Several years ago, best buddies John Finney, Bob Mardian and I took the Outrigger's four-man surfing canoe out into a six-foot-plus swell at Old Man's Bowl. John is a sweet guy with many years' experience as a champion canoe paddler. Though we're best friends, Bob Mardian is still my arch rival. We can argue about anything pertinent to our macho rivalry. We even argue about who is taller, even though we appear to be the same height. He refers to me as a "sawed-off Portagee" and I classify him as "rotund," as his girth nearly matches his height.

Out at Old Man's Bowl, we positioned ourselves in the perfect place to take off and ride a wave all the way across the channel. Unfortunately, a huge, close-out wave forced us into a late, almost no-paddle takeoff. The canoe went vertical, falling down the face of the wave. Amazingly, the bow of the canoe dug into the trough of the wave. As the canoe came to an abrupt halt, we were catapulted forward. It was an "Oh, sh--!" wipeout. Finney escaped unscathed, Mardian hit his leg and received a laceration, and my knee hit the 'iako (part of the outrigger connecting to the canoe). The impact almost tore off my leg.

With the help of John and Bob, we all returned to shore. Later the doctor said, "Ouch!"

Our days of bravado canoe surfing were over.

1967

OUTRIGGER CANOE RACING TACTICS

WHEN YOU ARE BEHIND IN A RACE, take a chance. That was my belief. If you are ahead, play it safe. In this race (page 70 bottom) about fifty years ago (racing koa canoes), I cut the corner a little too close and this rice-bowl wave nailed us. The crew did an excellent job of holding the *ama* down and we did not flip over. Instead, the wave pushed us sideways. We recovered enough to finish the race.

One of the untold rules of paddling is that if you win, it's because the crew paddled swiftly and surely. If you lose, it usually is because the steersman messed up.

That is what paddlers have been telling me for years.

1968

THE OUTRIGGER AND HUI NALU CANOE CLUBS

I MADE SOME BRASH REMARKS in a magazine regarding the Hawai'i Surfing Association (HSA) and a respected vintage surfer of yesteryear, Sam Reid. Back then, in 1968, I did not surf in HSA contests and hence was not rated in their system. I surfed only in major international competitions. My résumé reflects my record. At the time Hawai'i's surfing leaders, led by the well-respected Wally Froiseth, were picking a team to represent the Islands for the world contest. The HSA opposed including me as a member of the Hawaiian team because I wasn't rated by them. Fortunately, I was still included on the Hawai'i team, went to the world contest and competed successfully. My brash remarks were prompted by the HSA's opposition to me. I reacted strongly.

Regarding Sam Reid, I recall an article in a surfing magazine in which he more or less pitted Outrigger Canoe Club against Hui Nalu in such a manner that it shed an unfavorable light on the Outrigger. Naturally, being an Outrigger surfer and paddler, I rose to our club's defense. Sam also made the mistake of claiming that Hui Nalu had started in 1908, but documents at the Hawai'i State Archives clearly show that Hui Nalu wasn't registered until 1911. Sam Reid, in my opinion, needlessly drove a race-based wedge between the two clubs.

For the record, I did paddle for Hui Nalu for a number of years. Our Hui Nalu senior men's crew was special and won many races. Nainoa Thompson stroked, followed by Kala Kukea in the number two position, Bruce Blankenfield in three, George Kissner in four and Myron Thompson in the fifth position. I steered. The crew was exceptional and, on occasion, made paddling an ethereal experience.

I am so sick of the needless *haole*-versus-locals confrontation that sometimes permeates our local culture. It is worse nowadays. I am proud of both Outrigger and Hui Nalu based on the grandeur of their athletes and their accomplishments. They are historical clubs.

I hope this explains my terse words in 1968.

1975

THE LAST HAWAIIAN PADDLE

IT WAS 1975. I had paddled in a number of Moloka'i outrigger canoe races, beginning in 1966 (we never even made it to the finish that year). The official name of the race back then was not "Moloka'i Ho'e" but simply the Moloka'i to O'ahu Canoe Race. The event was, as it is now, the world championship of outrigger canoe racing. I'm proud of my forty-five-year-old son, Heath, who finished seventh in a very competitive international field of about 100 teams several years ago. He has raced in twenty-two Moloka'i's; I competed in only twelve.

In 1975 our Outrigger teams had done well in previous years' races and we certainly qualified as one of the favorites. Three complete teams from Tahiti were rumored to be entered in the race for the first time. Hawaiian clubs were very interested in the Tahitians. It seems that they were paddling with smaller teardrop-shaped blades with a much higher stroke count of about 60 SPM (strokes per minute). We considered that a sprint and figured they would never last. Our Outrigger team, as I am sure was true with other Hawai'i teams, was looking forward to the challenge.

The Hawaiian teams raced with a traditional blade and stroke as we had done throughout the history of twentieth-century canoe racing in Hawai'i. The stroke was the same my father had used in the 1930s. Hawaiian paddles were big oval-shaped blades. We paddled at about 42 SPM and took it up to 44 to 46 SPM for sprints. It was quite arduous pulling large paddles. Our stroke was very long. We would bend deep with our chests almost to the gunnels, reaching out in front, and pull the cumbersome blade to past our hips. It was pretty and rhythmic. "Pretty and rhythmic" was soon to become obsolete. I wanted to make a statement and had my pal Kimo Austin make me a traditional koa paddle. Racing paddles at the time were made of lighter woods. I would steer with the koa blade for the forty miles.

There were about thirty-five teams entered in the 1975 race. As usual, most crews camped out at Hale O Lono, a small man-made harbor in the southwest lee of Moloka'i. Each team had a larger change boat and many had a smaller chase boat for drops and recovery.

Outrigger racing canoes have six seats. For many distance races there are nine paddlers on a team. Hence there are periodic changes in which relieving paddlers are dropped on course in front of the racing canoe and as the team paddles by, several paddlers jump out and the relief paddlers haul themselves in. The object is to change without slowing the canoe much. It's a difficult maneuver for several paddlers to jump out of a fast-moving canoe in turbulent seas while their replacements climb in. Changes are a big part of the race.

The starting line for the race was right outside the harbor and about three miles to La'au Point at the end of Moloka'i landfall. The approximately forty-mile race ended in front of the Moana Hotel on Waikīkī Beach. The Kaiwi Channel is famous for several reasons, including usually being very rough with groundswells and brisk trades.

Being successful in the Moloka'i race requires a lot of finesse as well as paddling ability. Besides paddling the boat fast, of course, efficient changes, optimum use of swells and a number of other factors play a part in the success of what seems like an uncomplicated sport.

In 1975, we jockeyed for position at the starting line, curious about our Tahitian competitors. Our traditional rivals were Waikīkī Surf Club, Healani and Hui Nalu.

It's no secret that reaching La'au Point as a leader was important. That's because all the chase boats are required to stay behind the racing crews until La'au, when the first change can be made. The teams go all out in this initial leg of the race—to get into the lead and avoid the wake and chaos of all the escort boats. Part of my job as steersman was to make sure our crew blew off the line first. A huge dynamite explosion on shore started the race. To our astonishment, within the first mile the Tahitians already had a 100-yard lead. Our Outrigger team was fighting with Surf Club for fourth. So it was when we hit La'au Point and entered the channel that the Tahitians had what seemed to be a quarter-mile lead. I remember thinking it was going to be a long day.

Our redemption was the channel. The swell was big and the trade winds were brisk. Hooray! Looking ahead I could see the Tahitian boats snaking and not holding a solid straight course in the stubborn channel. Nevertheless, they were ahead—way ahead. Due to the tides that day, it was smartest to aim right for Diamond Head rather than Koko Head and to try to ride tidal currents into Waikīkī. The Tahitians were on a zigzag course to Diamond Head. I figured that by staying behind them and just paddling they would be difficult to pass. Surely their steersman would be smart enough to "cover" us as we got close and tried to pass them. We took a northerly course. If we could get high on them by a mile or two and stay within striking distance, we could turn downwind and surf past them.

The Tahitians were paddling fast indeed, but they were all over the place. About three-fourths of the way to O'ahu we were what appeared to be abreast of the lead Tahitian canoe, but way north. Surf Club was behind us. It was then that we made our move and took a new line "downhill." We aimed to be in front of the lead Tahitian boat. Our crew was strong, steady and relentless. We finally reached the Tahitian pack and surfed into first. We never looked back and after five hours, thirty-nine minutes and seven seconds of paddling we crossed the finish line in record time. I had a difficult time getting out of our racing canoe, the venerable *Kakina*.

Our Outrigger Canoe Club crew consisted of Brant Ackerman, Mark Buck, Tom Connor, Tim Guard, Paul MacLaughlin, Don Mailer, Mike Rodrigues and me.

We were proud. As fate would have it, that was the last time that contending canoe teams used the traditional Hawaiian blade in canoe racing.

Now, forty long years later, my koa blade hangs on my wall. It is the last Hawaiian paddle.

In the 1967 Moloka'i to O'ahu Canoe Race, after checking with an official on the rules, I steered inside the reef at Diamond Head, beating several canoes that remained outside. Race officials changed the rule the following year.

Politics Is Not a Dirty Word

1984-1990

STATE REPRESENTATIVE,
STATE OF HAWAI'I

ONE OF MY MOST MEMORABLE EPISODES as a member of Hawai'i's House of Representatives was quite intriguing beyond the confines of the legislative process. As fate would have it, I was advised by a very honest member of the state's fledging sheriffs' department about broad corruption and empire building at taxpayer expense. The corruption was managed by a clever operative who somehow had gained power, and whose *modus operandi* included holding warrants and fixing traffic violations for friends and politicians, assigning cases of friends to a few sympathetic judges, and building a quasi-military police force in the state judiciary. This included "deputizing" friends and giving them permits to carry guns.

I decided to blow the whistle on it all. However, none of my colleagues would join in the effort. I held a press conference that started a yearlong investigation that resulted in major legislation that took the sheriffs' department out of the judiciary and into the executive branch of state government, where it belonged. The operative responsible for the corruption eventually was indicted by a very independent city prosecutor, Chuck Marsland. His political hacks in the Legislature gave the culprit an unprecedented and very generous pay raise to enhance his "high three" retirement.

My whistleblowing resulted in telephoned death threats to my elderly father. The caller told my dad that I would be shot unless I backed off.

I was scared. I remembered the state senator who had been shot in his own carport in 1970. A relative of the alleged shooter worked as a high-ranking sheriff, a fact of which I was not so diplomatically reminded. I went to Doug Gibb, Honolulu's chief of police, and asked for protection. He said the best he could do was give me a very rare license to bear a concealed weapon. I wore a gun for more than a year.

This incident was researched and documented by Ian Lind, director of the advocacy group Common Cause Hawai'i, and Stirling Morita vigorously reported the details in the *Honolulu Star-Bulletin*. Very few remember this incident in the mid-1980s. But I sure do!

1990

MEMORABLE MOMENTS WITH PRESIDENT GEORGE H.W. BUSH

Y EARS AGO I had the pleasure of greeting President George H.W. Bush at his arrival at Hickam Air Force Base in Honolulu. An entourage of local political leaders rode a bus from the Hilton Hawaiian Village in Waikīkī to greet the president. Then we were going to load up and follow the president's limo back to the village to attend a rally for Hawai'i Congressional candidate Pat Saiki.

As fate would have it, several years earlier I had sat at a Denver Broncos football game with then Vice President Bush and his wife, Barbara. What a loving and pleasant couple! The real Camelot!

The president and Hawai'i Republican leaders all stood on the tarmac at Hickam and chatted for a few minutes. The president's limo pulled up next to us and it was time to go. Elected officials were to get back on our bus and follow the president's entourage to the Hilton Hawaiian Village.

President Bush looked at me and said, "Hey, Fred, you want to ride with me?" You know I was elated to receive the invitation. Frank Fasi, then the mayor of Honolulu, was within earshot and quickly asked the president if he could join us. Gracious President Bush said, "Yes." While we proceeded

(Continued on page 73)

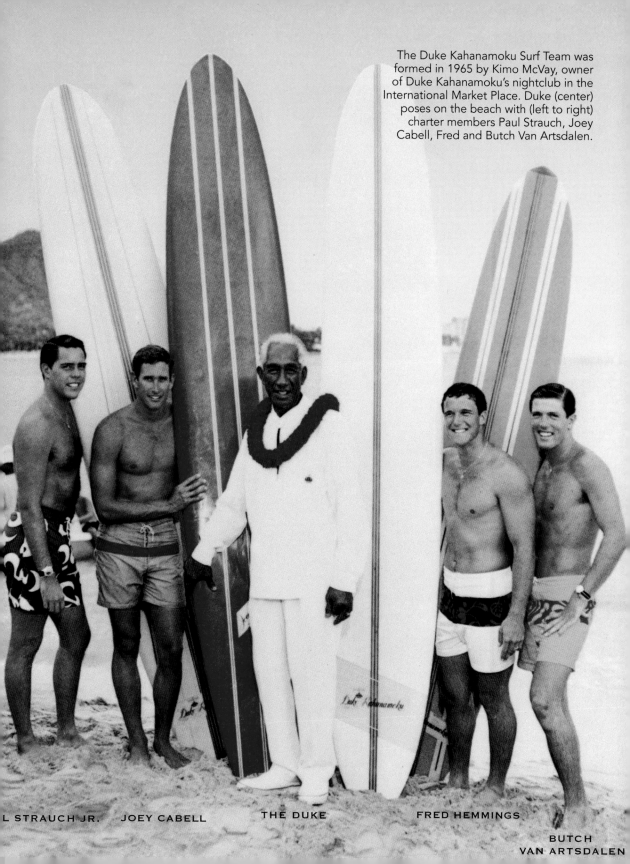

The Duke Kahanamoku Surf Team was formed in 1965 by Kimo McVay, owner of Duke Kahanamoku's nightclub in the International Market Place. Duke (center) poses on the beach with (left to right) charter members Paul Strauch, Joey Cabell, Fred and Butch Van Artsdalen.

L STRAUCH JR.   JOEY CABELL   THE DUKE   FRED HEMMINGS

BUTCH VAN ARTSDALEN

In 1958 Fred (center) competed in the junior men's division at a Mākaha surf meet against (left to right) winner Nappy Napoleon, Paul Strauch, Don Stroud and Wayne Miyata.

The Hemmings men (left to right: father Big Fred, brother Mark, Fred and brother Aka) pose in an early ad for the first Jams shorts.

On Lanikai Beach with a
direct line to God.

Mākaha, late 1960s: To help test the market for a new line of Jams pants, Fred wears a pair created for him by Jams founder Dave Rochlen. Right: Riding the first man-made wave at Big Surf water park, Tempe, Arizona.

Left to right: Fred, Paul Strauch, Duke and Butch Van Artsdalen pose for a 1966 Duke Kahanamoku Surf Team photo in Los Angeles.

Soul arch, riding "Big Red"
at Waimea Bay in 1965.

With Fred steering, the 1968 Outrigger Canoe Club team wields traditional Hawaiian big blades. Here the crew is recovering after a large swell rolled over them.

Fred in a casual turn on his favorite board, "Blue Max," at the Mākaha contest in 1966.

Riding one of board shaper Dick Brewer's first big wave guns, Fred makes a gouging turn at the Mākaha Bowl on a big day in 1964.

Fred and Denver Broncos owner Pat Bowlen canoe surfing at Old Man's Bowl ca. 1974.

Randy Rarick (left) and Fred ride a glassy Mākaha wall in the famous "swell of the century" in 1969.

First Lady Laura Bush, Lydia and Fred meet in 2006 at a White House dinner for backers of a Northwestern Hawaiian Islands marine sanctuary.

Fred, Lydia and son Gordon bid aloha to the Portuguese sailing ship *Sagres* in the waters off Waikīkī Beach.

Fred and grandchildren in 2010: (left to right) Trevor, Leo, Kiera, Hanna, Merrick and Eleanor.

Daughter Meaghan and granddaughter Kiera in 2014.

Son-in-law Andy Lautenbach and Fred's daughter Kaui Hart Hemmings with their children, Eleanor Hart Lautenbach and Eyosiyas "Leo" Andrew Lautenbach.

Son Heath Hemmings and daughter-in-law Dr. Daphne Hemmings with their three children, Trevor Ian Hemmings, Merrick Heath Hemmings and Hanna Lillian Hemmings, in 2015.

Fred solo canoe surfing
at Waikīkī.

PACIFIC
PADDLER

August 2000

The August 2000 cover of *Pacific Paddler* magazine captures Fred, Billy Balding and Kimo Austin about to be pummeled.

ne magazine for paddlers by paddl

in a heavily guarded motorcade on the totally cleared roadways to Waikīkī, Mayor Fasi talked profusely about politics. When I finally had a chance to get in a word, I simply stated, "Mr. President, I hope you are going to be tough in Iraq." I never will forget the next couple of moments. The president's whole mood changed from lighthearted to very serious. He looked right at me and said, "Yes, I am." I did not bother him with any more inquiries, sensing that the subject was delicate and surely top secret.

History will show that Operation Desert Storm, then in the planning stages, and the possibility of sending thousands of American and coalition troops into mortal battle was obviously weighing heavily on the president's mind. It was a dramatic moment in the car ride to Waikīkī and in a curious way a historic moment for me.

History was made soon afterward, when Operation Desert Storm liberated Kuwait in one of the astonishing military engagements in history. It was swift and sure.

Attending a Denver Broncos game with then Vice President George H.W. Bush and old friends Kerry Komatsubara and John Finney.

Greeting President George H.W. Bush in Honolulu in 1990.

1994

CANDIDATE FOR LIEUTENANT GOVERNOR

THE INDOMITABLE **PAT SAIKI** ran for governor in 1994. I was honored to be her candidate for lieutenant governor. Ben Cayetano was the Democratic nominee. Frank Fasi, unable to get the Democrat or the Republican nomination, formed his own Best Party and ran with the jovial Danny Kaleikini as his running mate. That split the opposition vote and Ben won with only about thirty-seven percent of the general election vote. Hawai'i politics is always interesting! And this political cartoon by John S. Pritchett is fun, isn't it!

2006

A COLLEGE OF SPORTS

I wrote the following in 2006 when I was a state senator.

Hawai'i is the water sports capital of the world and a premier multisports venue. The evidence is there to verify that claim. It makes eminent sense to initiate a major College of Sports at the University of Hawai'i that would enable students to earn a college degree in sports. Sounds incredulous? Let's explore the idea.

What's the justification for something so bold and different, especially in view of the fact that some view sports as the antithesis of institutions of higher learning? But really what a university is all about is educating young people to enter the marketplace of life and gain productive employment in order to be contributing members of our society. This alone is a major justification to establish a College of Sports at the University of Hawai'i.

Sports are a hidden industry in Hawai'i. Sports contribute significantly to the health and economic welfare of the state of Hawai'i. Let's take a brief inventory of some of Hawai'i's major events.

We all know that the Honolulu Marathon not only promotes personal health but also has a tremendous economic impact on our state. Several years ago *Condé Nast Traveler* magazine published its list of the fifty best golf resorts in North America, Hawai'i and the Caribbean. Hawai'i dominated the list with sixteen; three of Hawai'i's alluring golf courses were in the top five. Would it be safe to say that we have more world-class golf courses than any other state, or nearly any other nation in the world?

Our water sports are unparalleled. Hale'iwa is the surfing capital of the world. The North Shore of O'ahu is revered in the world of surfing. And trust me, surfing is a multibillion-dollar sports industry with a professional circuit littered with Hawai'i athletes who excel in the competitions.

Windsurfing and kitesurfing have replaced sugar as a viable industry in the town of Pa'ia, Maui. Pa'ia is considered one of the meccas of windsurfing.

Hawai'i sailing is renowned in spite of the fact that our state lacks adequate mooring space and infrastructure. As you remember, the fabled American yachtsman Dennis Conner trained for the America's Cup in Hawai'i.

Hawai'i's international billfish tournament in Kona on the Big Island of Hawai'i is one of the world's best and oldest.

The Ironman Triathlon is the world's premier triathlon. In fact, the triathlon sport was inaugurated in Hawai'i.

Hawaiian outrigger canoe racing is following the path of its sister sport, surfing, as an international sport. There is even an outrigger canoe race on the Hudson River in New York.

Hawai'i's land sports are equally notable. The University of Hawai'i regularly achieves national prominence in volleyball, football, baseball and basketball, which are mainstay sports on the continent. They do play a role in all our lives here in the Islands, especially in our high schools.

Soccer is the number one international sport and is growing rapidly in Hawai'i.

In spite of the lack of adequate public infrastructure to host better and more sports activities, Hawai'i still is one of the great playgrounds of the world and certainly is the watersports capital of the world.

Do sports and sports related events generate more income for the state economy than, let's say, agriculture? Think about it. As you know there is a Department of Agriculture in state government, but no Department of Sports. I am not advocating a Department of Sports. It would make more sense to have tax dollars spent on sports infrastructure and let the marketplace of entrepreneurs and sportsmen and women further develop the local sports industry.

My friend Pat Bowlen, owner of the Denver Broncos, said he is inundated on a regular basis by people seeking employment in the professional football business, yet they do not have degrees in "sports." Many pro athletes took "maintenance" courses in college to remain eligible to play. Do you remember the jest about the outstanding pro athlete majoring in basket weaving in college? Many retired players end up employed in the sports industry.

I am proposing that students at the University of Hawai'i have an opportunity to obtain a bachelor's degree from a College of Sports at the University of Hawai'i. It would make sense to offer three major areas of discipline at the College of Sports. Students would have to take some accredited course in each discipline to receive a bachelor's degree in sports.

The first area of study would be sports management, coaching and sports facility management. In the future, this would include, as potential students, thousands, if not hundreds of thousands of coaches, athletic directors and facility managers who are employed nationwide to receive a college degree in their specific area of employment, sports.

The second school of discipline within the College of Sports would be sports medicine, science and technology. Sports medicine is particularly interesting because sports and outdoor recreation are the primary reason that Hawai'i also has earned the title of the Health State. Many Hawai'i citizens are healthy because we are not couch potatoes. You can see it from the early morning joggers until late in the evening with sports enthusiasts using the ocean and land for recreation and health. Many people are employed in various aspects of the health and sports medicine industry. This includes everyone from medical doctors, rehabilitation trainers and technicians to research and development experts. Each should have a degree in sports.

The final discipline that the College of Sports would feature is sports marketing, merchandising, communication and history. It wasn't too long ago that the only way to purchase a pair of surfing trunks was from a little old Japanese man in Wai'anae named M. Nii, or from the famous Taki's in Waikīkī. Now the surf apparel industry is a multibillion-dollar international business with corporations traded on the major stock exchanges of the world. Sports merchandising and marketing are pervasive in the economy, not only in Hawai'i, but around the world.

Sports are major entertainment, especially on television. The Super Bowl is consistently the highest rated television event in America. In the arena of sports history, Hawai'i is the wellspring of sports. For instance, few know that the first beach volleyball games were played on the beach at Waikīkī early last century. (By the way, it is time to refurbish the idle Natatorium as a world-class volleyball arena.) The genesis of the famous triathlon is here in Hawai'i. Windsurfing traces its roots to Hawai'i. Of course surfing as we know it originated in ancient Hawai'i. Televised coverage of the Triple Crown of Surfing is seen around the world.

Doesn't it make sense that young people seeking an economic future in sports related industries have a degree that coincides with their area of employment? I say, "Yes."

The University of Hawai'i could have the premier College of Sports in the nation. Students would receive a four-year bachelor's degree and then contribute to society through gainful employment in the multifaceted sports industry. It makes eminent sense.

2006

PAPAHĀNAUMOKUĀKEA
MARINE NATIONAL MONUMENT

Some background on the establishment of the Papahānaumokuākea Marine National Monument.

The concept of creating some sort of a marine reserve for the northwestern islands of the Hawaiian Archipelago was discussed in Congress for several years. Hawai'i congressman Ed Case was an early advocate. As fate would have it, the Northwestern Hawaiian Islands were part of my 25th State Senate District. Congressman Case's legislation was stalled in Congress. I supported the concept of creating the world's largest marine reserve and proposed it to Hawai'i's governor, Linda Lingle. After vetting the proposal with community leaders, Governor Lingle took the proposal to President George W. Bush.

President Bush sent the chairman of the White House Council on Environmental Quality, James Connaughton, to Hawai'i, where we joined him and a small delegation on a journey to Midway Atoll. We flew at a low altitude over most of the islands of the archipelago and landed on Midway, which actually consists of two atolls. I believe the highest elevation is sixteen feet and only forty-two people live there. There must be a million gooney birds (albatrosses) living among these forty-two inhabitants, which makes landing there a little difficult. The island is maintained primarily as an emergency landing field for transpacific flights and for the United States Coast Guard. It's a lonely place. During World War II it was a major battleground with many thousands of troops and Naval facilities. The Battle of Midway is historic and marked the turning point for America's eventual victory over imperial Japan.

Soon after our visit to Midway, President George W. Bush and First Lady Laura Bush, who is a most gracious woman, invited me to a White House dinner attended by Hawai'i and other proponents of a Northwestern Hawaiian Islands sanctuary. It was a small group that gathered for a memorable meal after viewing, in the White House theater, Jean-Michel Cousteau's film, *The Voyage to Kure*. Michel, the son of the late underwater explorer Captain Jacques Cousteau, accompanied us on our trip to Midway.

We discussed the subject of creating the largest marine protected area in the world at the time. President Bush seemed very positive. James Connaughton should get the credit for putting together the details for the eventual presidential declaration. Two months after our dinner, in early 2006, I was again invited to the White House to attend the declaration ceremony for the new sanctuary. The ceremony was held in the East Room, which usually is reserved for more formal press conferences and official ceremonies. Due to the magnitude of the declaration, however, more than 200 members of the world's press corps were present. I sat with Governor Lingle, members of Congress and other leaders of world environmental organizations. President Bush signed the presidential declaration creating the sanctuary. I was honored to receive a ceremonial copy of the declaration. After the ceremony, as I was leaving, President Bush said loudly, "See ya, Senator Hemmings," and waved goodbye.

Lydia and I meet with Governor Linda Lingle and President George W. Bush at the White House.

Soon after, First Lady Laura Bush led the search for a culturally appropriate name, hence the long but correct Hawaiian name, Papahānaumokuākea. The name celebrates the union of two Hawaiian ancestors: Papahānaumoku, the earth mother goddess; and Wākea, the sky father who gave rise to the Hawaiian Archipelago, the taro plant and the Hawaiian people.

I hope future generations will know and appreciate what President Bush accomplished—the creation of the largest contiguous, fully protected conservation area under U.S. jurisdiction and one of the largest marine conservation areas in the world.

President Bush and Governor Lingle deserve so much credit for the creation of Papahānaumokuākea. I felt honored to be part of the process.

2007

ENTERPRISE ZONES

January 9, 2007

To Constituents:

Senator Fred Hemmings has developed legislation for special enterprise zones. This legislation is to develop and provide economic incentives and to streamline permitting for Hawai'i to seize the opportunity to develop space launch enterprise zones, renewable energy enterprise zones or maritime industry enterprise zones.

In short, the southeast coast of the Big Island of Hawai'i is one of the best places in the world, if not the best, for equatorial and polar launches of space vehicles and satellites. Hawai'i is best suited for solar and other renewable energy, yet we are the state most dependent on fossil fuels. Hawai'i's harbors are in the doldrums. Hawai'i is an island state sadly lacking in mooring space in our harbors.

Senator Hemmings feels these are major opportunities that have been unrealized in the past.

Your comments and assistance in making these initiatives real in the twenty-first century will be most beneficial and appreciated.

2008

MARTIN LUTHER KING

WHILE WAITING IN THE LOBBY of a Capitol Hill hotel several years ago, I was reading a wonderful book, *Letters of a Nation*. At the same time, a group of elderly African-American men were gathering outside a nearby conference room. On a blank page in the back of my book I wrote them the following letter, which they never saw.

Dear Men,

In you I see America's promises coming true. Your eyes reflect the spirit that has borne your people through great pain and labor to a new life. You are men of strong character as seen in your garb and the sense of pride you obviously take in how you look. You are gentlemen. Your merriment and laughter is contagious.

I am a white man who knows not firsthand of the prejudice you have endured in the years gone by. I am from Hawai'i, where the specter of the racism that plagued you was absent. The injustices of your journey I do know. I know the book of America's history is stained with your tears.

Great men and women have led us through the pain, sorrow and folly that humankind can sadly inflict on itself. You and our nation have endured. Our nation has also been blessed by the better spirits of humanity.

In the pantheon of America's greatest leaders is the beloved Martin Luther King. His legacy is your promised land. Please, brothers, see the America of the future, not the dark clouds of the past. Stand shoulder to shoulder with all. Out of many we are one. That is the dream come true.

Aloha,
Fred Hemmings
A friend from Hawai'i

2010

THE UNITED STATES MILITARY

AS A CITIZEN OF THE UNITED STATES, I have the greatest admiration for the United States military. The men and women who serve often pay the ultimate price for our freedom for which we all should be eternally grateful. As a state senator, I often would assist the military command in Hawai'i in fighting ill-conceived legislation that was not in the best interests of the Army, Air Force, Marine and Navy commands in Hawai'i. As a result, I became close personal friends with numerous flag officers, including those who led the Pacific commands. On numerous occasions I was invited to special opportunities, such as being tail-hooked flying onto the *Carl Vincent* aircraft carrier and spending thirty-six hours, much of it underwater, on a fast attack submarine, the *U.S.S. Birmingham.*

God bless the men and women of the United States military, who serve this country and the cause of freedom.

I wrote the above on Memorial Day 2010, when I was a state senator. I am so proud that my stepson, Gordon, is a stalwart scholar, athlete and leader at the Air Force Academy. He wants to be an aeronautical engineer and pilot. I want him to be on the first expedition to Mars.

My wife, Lydia, and stepson Gordon Kowalkowski at the Air Force Academy.

2010

THE SAGRES

THE **PORTUGUESE** were the great navigators of the age of exploration. If you are interested, look up Prince Henry the Navigator, who founded a famed fifteenth-century cartography and navigation institute in the Portuguese city of Sagres.

In 2010, the beautiful Portuguese sailing ship *Sagres* stopped in Honolulu before heading west to Japan. My wife, Lydia, and I, along with Portuguese counsel general John Henry Felix, were honored to be guests at a luncheon hosted by Captain Propencea in his stateroom on the ship. The day before, I had taken him and the first officer out to catch a few waves in an outrigger canoe.

I suggested to Captain Propencea that, upon departure, he motor up to the Diamond Head buoy and after coming about, unfurl the *Sagres's* lofty sails and sail along Waikīkī Beach before turning west for the long journey to Japan. He agreed, but only if we paddled out in a canoe to say goodbye as he sailed by. The next day Lydia, my son Gordon and I paddled out to the deep blue. It was truly awe-inspiring to see the majestic *Sagres* under full sail bearing down upon us. We passed within yards of the *Sagres* and Captain Propencea and his crew shouted goodbye. We bid farewell to the *Sagres*, with our aloha.

As fate would have it, local photographer Twain Newhart was paddling his one-man canoe nearby. Twain had his camera with him and happened to be in the perfect position to take a photo. It couldn't have been planned any better. Soon afterward I was in Washington, D.C., and had lunch with the Portuguese ambassador to the U.S. I presented him with an enlargement of Twain's epic photo. You can see it on page 66.

2013

U.S. SENATOR DANIEL K. INOUYE

YEARS AGO I gave U.S. Senator Daniel Inouye a framed surfing photo for his office in Washington, D.C. Upon his death the photo was placed in his legacy fund. The photo was returned to me eventually and hangs proudly in my home on Oʻahu. It is inscribed with a plaque designating it, "Daniel K. Inouye Legacy Fund." I wrote a letter of thanks to Irene Hirano Inouye.

February 23, 2013

Irene Hirano Inouye
President
U.S.-Japan Council
1819 L Street, N.W., #200
Washington, D.C. 20036

Dear Irene,

I will treasure and prominently display the returned surfing photo from Senator Inouye's Legacy Fund.

I feel Senator Daniel K. Inouye was the best elected official in the history of Hawaiʻi. It is a bold statement based on merit. Though I am of a different political persuasion I can freely say Senator Inouye was my hero. He loved Hawaiʻi and made our Islands a better place. I would be most willing and honored to do all I can to preserve his memory and legacy. It is said we should learn from our history. Senator Inouye taught us much.

Warmest aloha,
Fred Hemmings
An old surfer

Musings, Pets and "All Kine Stuff"

1975

THE BABY AIRLIFT

I**T WAS 1975** and Viet Cong forces were on the outskirts of Saigon, on the verge of conquering the city.

It was no secret that the Communists would "purge" South Vietnam of all those who did not subscribe to their totalitarian state. Many innocent citizens would be killed, tortured or imprisoned. As with the Communist takeovers in other countries, there could very well be a pogrom and as a result, a massive evacuation was underway. Some South Vietnamese were risking their lives escaping on flimsy boats; they were that desperate.

Charitable organizations were rescuing children from orphanages. These children would be evacuated to America and made available for adoption in an effort called Operation Babylift, or the baby airlift. Some Vietnamese children already were adopted and had parents waiting for them. Tragically one baby airlift plane crashed, killing all on board.

Among those who were assisting with this mass evacuation was an American philanthropist who chartered a Pan Am 747 to carry children on the long journey to the U.S. My name was on a list of Red Cross volunteers to help in emergencies. I received a call to come to Honolulu International Airport to help care for the children while the Pan Am flight was on the ground. The plane had been on an eighteen-hour journey and the caregivers on board were wiped out with exhaustion. I would find out why.

We boarded the plane to find a sea of crying babies and older children ranging in age from several months to seven or eight years old. It was a mess. After about a half hour of changing diapers and cleaning babies, I came upon a bassinet with what appeared to be a six- to eight-month-old child. She was howling and her arms reached up while her eyes pleaded for me to embrace her. Those eyes pierced my soul. Somehow there was a connection. As I held her she clutched me so very tightly. After caring for her, I went to secure her in the bassinet, but she wouldn't let me go and howled with anguish. I could not put her down. I spent the remaining time helping other children while somehow holding her. I should say she held me. I learned from this baby how important and nourishing it is for a child to be embraced both emotionally and physically.

When it came time for the plane to leave Honolulu for Seattle, one of the babylift volunteers in charge asked me if I would stay and continue to assist. Pan Am would fly me back. I asked the woman to make a few phone calls for me and I stayed on the plane. Most of the flight was spent moving from child to child tending to their needs, which included mostly bottle feeding and changing diapers. But my little girl stayed in my arms for the entire flight.

We arrived in Seattle, where many anxious adoptive parents waited at the windows beyond Customs. When it was time for me to let go of my little girl, it was very difficult.

1980s-2015

THE CHAIN SAW CHRONICLES
AND OTHER YARD WORK CALAMITIES

WHO KNOWS WHY? I always have enjoyed yard work. It might be because of my anal-retentive proclivity to make sure everything is in its place and manicured. As a result of my yardman "hobby" over the years, I acquired all the necessary equipment, including a powerful chain saw to keep in the trailer along with many other tools of the trade. I towed the trailer behind my rider mower; we had a big yard. At the time our remote home was at the base of the Nu'uanu Pali in the rain forest. It seems that sometimes I was inclined to try to tame the entire forest.

Being a Portuguese yardman is not easy and comes with hard work, some fun and some peril. Here are a few of my yardman stories.

Pali Highway Work Crew, 2005

On a windy, rainy New Year's morning in 2005, my wife, Lydia, was driving on Pali Highway when she came upon a fallen tree that blocked most of the townbound lanes to Honolulu. Traffic slowed as commuters drove over and around branches of the fallen tree. Lydia called me and stated explicitly, "Put on your work clothes and grab your chain saw. A tree is blocking Pali Highway and no one is here to clean it up."

I hustled up there and found a City and County of Honolulu truck with two workers who just had arrived standing with Lydia. They had a scrawny chain saw, but it didn't work. I revved up my 18-inch chain saw—I'm no Paul Bunyan, but at least I had the right equipment. The two city workers told my wife that they were going back to the base yard to get another chain saw. It took only about twenty minutes for me to chew up the fallen tree while Lydia threw the branches over the side of the road. We noticed a camera operator taking a video of us working on the other side of Pali Highway. Local television news that night reported that an unidentified couple had cleared the road.

A police officer showed up, dutifully turned on his light and stood directing traffic while Lydia and I finished up the work of getting the tree off the road. Don't you just love how police officers do everything to help, like waving traffic by? Sometimes they use both hands.

As we were finishing our work, the officer asked if our crew, which consisted of Lydia and me, could go up to the Pali Lookout on-ramp and clear another fallen tree. I figured out later that the police officer assumed that Lydia was the foreman and I was her crew. He was correct about that. We looked at each and almost burst out laughing, but gamely said, "Sure." I don't think the police officer understood that we were not employed by the City and County of Honolulu. At the time I was employed by the state senate.

Death by Tree, 2015

It was October of 2015. We lived on a remote road above the Pali Golf Course. My son and daughter-in-law's home and our home were the only houses on the road. The homes were about a quarter-mile off of Pali Highway, above Castle Junction. They were surrounded by a rain forest.

Having cut down most of the weed trees on our property, in the spirit of public service I frequently groomed the road leading to our house. This day I was perched on a little incline on the side of the road and was cutting down, as I had done so many times before, a weed tree. It was about eight inches in diameter. As usual, when the tree started to crack and fall, I stepped away, holding my chain saw. The tree thundered to the ground in such a manner that it kicked back. The trunk of the fallen tree hit me in the left side of my chest and shoulder, literally blowing me off my feet. You know how people sometimes say their lives flash before them if they think they're dying? That didn't happen to me. Rather, as I flew into the air, the thought flashed through my mind, *I have killed myself.*

I hit the ground and must have passed out. When I came to, the left side of my body, from my waist to my neck was tingling, and the pain in my ribs and one shoulder was excruciating. I told myself I was a tough guy and, as in the past, it would get better. Although any movement was painful, I put my right hand in the pocket of my jeans and retrieved my cell phone.

I called Lydia and said, "I'm hurt. Come home." Fortunately for me I had made friends with several homeless men living in the rain forest. One of them, Tony, ran down the hill when he heard the tree crash. Tony saw my crushed rib cage and my shoulder, which also appeared to be crushed. I tried to move, but he told me not to. Right then, Lydia and my granddaughter Hanna arrived. I instructed Lydia to move the car closer, help Tony lift me over the fallen tree, and take me to the hospital. Lydia agreed and dialed 911.

Through the years, Honolulu's daily newspapers had reported on my too-frequent yard work accidents. This time, barely conscious, I was more concerned with trying to avoid another embarrassing yard work story, and I didn't fully realize the extent of the damage done.

My son Heath arrived with my grandson Merrick. Heath, Tony and Lydia communicated with the emergency medical technicians who were en route. When they arrived they were able to get me on a stretcher, over the fallen tree and into the ambulance. The next thing I remember is being in the ambulance with Lydia on the way to The Queen's Medical Center emergency room, where, fortunately, my daughter-in-law Daphne Hemmings, M.D., was on duty.

I was in shock but eventually regained my composure somewhat. In the medical surgical unit, the staff told Lydia I had crushed seven ribs, punctured a lung and crushed a shoulder. The doctors decided not to send me to surgery to put in steel plates to reinforce my ribs. To control the pain, an anesthesiologist administered a spinal block. They injected interim pain killers for the procedures but missed the mark on the first attempt and made a second try.

Lydia was in the room all this time. She relayed to me later that while I was staring at the ceiling I told her, "Something's wrong." I was hooked up to one of those all-purpose monitors; Lydia looked at it and saw immediately that my heart rate was falling. She ran out of the room, calling out my room number and yelling that my heart was failing. When she reentered the room my heart had stopped completely.

I was lying there with wide open, glazed over eyes. Within seconds medical personnel filled the room. The charge nurse immediately jumped on me and administered CPR. This certainly did not help my broken ribs. Fortunately, however, I didn't know the difference. My heart started to beat again. Someone later explained to me that the excessive amount of painkillers had slowed down and stopped my heart. I had died, but only for a few seconds.

And that's my story of death by chain saw.

P.S. Even before I was discharged from the hospital, Lydia had sold my chain saw on eBay.

My Ajinomoto Story

In case you don't know, Ajinomoto is a Japanese seasoning similar to salt.

In the 1980s, we were living in a large house with an equally large yard in Maunawili. I was by myself at home and planned on catching a flight to Maui that afternoon to participate in the Hāna Relays, a six-member team, fifty-two-mile running relay race from Kahului to Hāna. I figured I could quickly mow my large lawn with a mulching mower before driving to the airport, so I put on my jogging shoes and shorts. As I was mowing, I came to a section of the yard with a steep incline. I was pushing the mower downhill and then pulled it up to take another sweep when my feet slipped out from under me and kicked forward. Somehow in reaction, my arms lifted the mower up onto its front wheels. My right foot kicked the mower's high-speed blade. The mower dropped as I fell back on my 'ōkole.

As I looked down at the front of my mangled right shoe, the intense pain left no doubt I should get down the hill to Castle Medical Center. This was confirmed when I lifted up the front part of the canvas shoe and saw that I had filleted three toes on my right foot. The front of my foot, besides hurting big-time, felt wet with blood.

No one was home, I had no cell phone and I didn't want to drag myself into the house to call and wait for an ambulance. I thought it would be faster to hop into my car and drive the half mile down to Castle, which I proceeded to do.

What often happens in accidents like this is that you go into shock and the pain abates. I managed to hop and limp into my car. As I drove I felt light-headed, like I was going to faint. I leaned my head against the car window and, with all the concentration I could muster, managed to drive to Castle's emergency room entrance. I hopped across the pavement, hit the black pad that opens the automatic doors to the ER, and then immediately fell forward and fainted.

Henceforth, Castle Medical Center, as usual, took care of me.

But that's not the full story. I have a bunch of tough guy friends and every time they got sick or injured, I'd call to harass them. "What's wrong, wimp?" I'd say. "Can't you take it?"

Naturally, upon hearing that I'd cut off my toes, they took the opportunity to respond in kind. One of the cleverest was my friend Kerry Komatsubara, who dubbed me Ajinomoto—as in "Ah-gee-no-more-toe." Another buddy called and said, "Lucky you, Fred. Now you can park in the "toe-away zone." And of course my buddy Pat Bowlen called from Colorado.

"I can't stop laughing," he said. "Are you hurt?"

"No shit, Sherlock," I answered, and he laughed even harder.

But my favorite dig was from David Hagino, who called to check in and ask me if my Portuguese name was "Freddie *Sans*-toes."

The Retaining Wall

I was mowing the lawn at the Pali house. To make a long story short, I fell off a three-foot-high retaining wall and bounced off the asphalt driveway. I hit the hip that had been replaced, the one with the titanium spike in my femur and a new socket. Once again, the pain told me I needed help. I was lying on the ground, unable to move, without a cell phone and no one else at home. Occasionally I called out for help, but to no avail. Finally, Lydia arrived on the scene, managed to load me into the car and took me to Castle Medical Center. After an x-ray the doctor told me how lucky I was that the titanium spike in my bone had stopped me from completely breaking the bone. Don't you just love how doctors try to put a positive spin on accidents? Somehow, I didn't feel very lucky.

I suppose these are the perils of being such a diligent and anal Portuguese yardman.

My Grand Finale Medical Story

Years after my first hip replacement operation, my doctor's instructions included not doing any exercise, to prevent any injury of my "new" hip. Feeling rather hearty after several weeks in recovery, I asked my doctor if I could ride a bike to exercise. I guess he thought I was going to ride a stationary exercise bike in a controlled environment. As I was grinding down Kainalu Road in Kailua on the bike path, a car suddenly came backing out of a driveway. Slamming on the front brake, I flew over the handlebars, bouncing into a shoulder roll. Later on, I looked back proudly on that adroit shoulder roll—rather than kissing the road face first. Fortunately, I did not injure my hip. Rather, the spill broke my collarbone and tore some tendons.

When that happens, the collarbone sticks up. It looks gnarly.

A Japanese gentleman driving down the road pulled over and offered to help. He threw my bike to the side of the road and loaded me into his car. Apparently he recognized me as his state senator. While driving me to—you guessed it—the Castle Medical Center emergency room, he dutifully informed me, "You know, I'm a Democrat." Maybe he felt I'd be grateful that a Democrat was driving me, a lowly Republican, to the emergency room. And yes, I was.

So now you know why I feel so at home and know so many of the staff at the Castle E.R. We are so lucky to have Castle Medical Center in Kailua. They are the best!

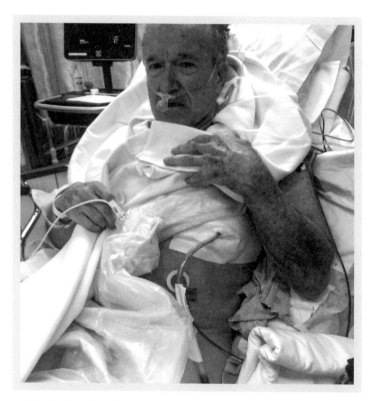

Hospitalized at The Queen's Medical Center in Honolulu after having been hit by a tree: seven crushed ribs, a punctured lung and a crushed shoulder. Ouch! The tube was draining fluid from my lungs.

1997

KERRY MULLIS

SO I'M STANDING WITH **MIKE DOYLE** and a few other well-known sixties-era surfers at a Scripps Institute surf event in San Diego. A stranger of about the same age walks up and proceeds to tell surf stories from years gone by. He looks to be in his fifties and is "stoked" like a teenage kid. It appeared that surfing was still the biggest thing in his life.

But not quite. After an exchange of surf stories and pleasantries, he bids us adieu and wanders off. I immediately ask Mike Doyle, "Who is that guy?" He says, "Oh, that's Kerry Mullis," like I certainly should know who Kerry Mullis is. Obviously, I don't.

Mike explains that the stoked middle-aged surfer, Kerry Mullis, won the Nobel Prize in Chemistry for his work in helping unravel DNA.

As it happens, I'm fascinated with DNA and its mysteries. So I had the pleasure of spending time with a surfing genius and didn't even know it.

1998

MIZZY

WHEN WE WERE LIVING in Maunawili I went to the Hawaiian Humane Society to adopt a cat. There I noticed a young pig in a cage. She was friendly and looked at me with wanting eyes. Who could say no to such a pretty face? I brought her home and named her Mizzy.

Mizzy adapted to the house quickly and let our two dogs know that she was not a pig to be trifled with. In fact, she quickly became the alpha female of the house. I often lay on the floor of our TV room with the dogs. The patio door was usually left open for the animals.

Mizzy would come in and chase the dogs out of the house and then return to relax with me. She was quite a pig and brought us many smiles.

1998

THE SUPER BOWL WITH JOHN ELWAY

Owner Pat Bowlen had arranged for the directors of the Denver Broncos to be on the field for the conclusion of the 1998 Super Bowl. I was fortunate to be with them. Pat is a part-time local boy. His two sons were born here. He and his wife, Annabelle, make an effort to spend time in Hawai'i every year. You wouldn't recognize Pat. In Denver he is dressed up like the owner of the Denver Broncos. While in Hawai'i he wears shorts with a T-shirt hanging out of his back pocket. In recent years, John and Janet Elway have joined us here in Hawai'i for a holiday.

This year his Super Bowl had an air of magic about it. We stepped out of the tunnel at the end of the field just as Terrell Davis scored the go-ahead touchdown. Yes, the crowd was intense, the pageantry once again had exceeded expectations and the world's most hyped athletic event was headed toward a tumultuous conclusion. But this Super Bowl was different. John Elway was the elixir of the magic that was in the air. A buddy, Al Balika, and I stood on the sideline at about the 35 as Green Bay started its attempt with less than two minutes left to march down the field to score. If anyone knew that a team could mount an epic drive in less than two minutes, it was John Elway. In fact, my most vivid memory is of Elway's magic in the waning minutes of a football game. It takes a special person to perform at his best with disaster looming only seconds away.

On Sunday Elway's entire career would be punctuated by the next minute or so. He stood several yards from us. This aging football warrior had his helmet on, ready in a second to run back on the field if needed. Elway's journey to this moment had started what seemed like a lifetime ago. This was Elway's destiny. He turned and started to walk toward Al and me. His head was bent, pensively staring at the ground as he walked. Who knew what he was thinking? As he raised his head he looked right at us. Our eyes met and without words, he said, "Hello." Then, in a flicker of a second, a spark of humanity passed between us. John Elway raised his head high and, looking at us, rolled his eyes skyward as if to say, "My God, can you believe this?"

Tears welled up in my eyes. John Elway turned and walked into the sidelines into football history.

2006

DUCKY

THIS IS DUCKY. Sorry about the lack of creativity in the name. Do you notice anything different about Ducky? He has only one leg. While living in Kailua next to the Kawai Nui Canal, I found Ducky as a very young hatchling. His leg had been almost severed at the hip. Without assistance, he would not have survived.

I took him into the house and very quickly amputated the severely injured leg. I put a dab of Super Glue on the exposed stem. He lived in a large box until the wound healed. Soon I could let him swim again, and no, Ducky did not swim in a circle.

Ducky had a large appetite. He fully recovered and grew up hearty and strong as a one-legged duck. I returned him to the canal. He would hop up regularly to get fed and be held.

I don't think Ducky knew he was a handicapped one-legged duck.

2008

MAKAI WAS PART ME

A FEW OF MY LIFE'S ADVENTURES—and misadventures—have been rather unique. Some may find this bizarre tale macabre. If you have a weak stomach or are otherwise delicate, you may not wish to read this.

It was 2003. My hip was completely worn out. At The Queen's Medical Center in Honolulu, a surgeon friend was going to replace the worn-out hip with a titanium joint. As always before an operation, I asked the doctor to tell me in detail what was going to be done. He explained that once I was under the anesthetic, they would roll me on my side, dislocate my hip, cut my flesh and saw off the very top of my femur bone—the part with the ball joint. They would then pound into the femur shank a shaft with a new ball on top, kind of like a trailer hitch. He also would fasten a new anchor point in the pelvis. In the customary visit by the surgeon before the operation I told him to please save the bone.

"No," he replied. "It's medical waste."

"Yes," I countered. The bone was part of my body and I wanted it.

After the surgery the doctor came to my room, checked me out and handed me a plastic baggie with the round head attached to a small part of the top of the femur bone.

Soon afterward, the bag with the bone in it ended up on the large desk in my Senate office at the State Capitol. It was a curious conversation piece. And no, I never made Portuguese bone soup!

Frequently I would bring my best four-legged friend, Makai, to the office. Makai was a precious Portuguese water dog—loyal, handsome and very smart, like most Portuguese! Makai would sit at the foot of my desk and always greeted visitors with merriment. You know how dogs can make you feel as though you are the greatest person in the world.

So one fine day after my hip operation, I was sitting at my desk with Makai, when I had to go to the men's room. I limped out of my office, telling my office manager that I'd be right back.

When I returned, Makai was lying in the middle of my office. He was chewing on my femur bone and in fact had already consumed most of it. It looked like a cue ball that had been eaten three-quarters of the way through; bone crumbs were on Makai's lips. I howled. Staff members came running in and laughed, although guardedly. After a few moments, I was laughing too.

And that's the grisly story of Makai and the femur. I may be the only person, of more than seven billion on the planet, who has been partially eaten by a dog and is still here to tell about it.

Makai, Mele the cat and me at the State Capitol.

2010

THE FIRST AND LAST BREATH

BACK IN THE 1970S, I was with a group of canoe paddlers on the Big Island. We were on the shore at Hōnaunau preparing for the first Liliʻuokalani Canoe Race to Kona. After the canoe was rigged we went for a paddle in vast Kealakekua Bay. We paddled across the bay to a white obelisk that marks a historic location. I jumped out of the canoe near shore while the crew watched me scramble up the rocks. This lonely obelisk on the shoreline marks the very spot where British explorer Captain James Cook was struck down and killed by Hawaiian warriors in 1779. It is the spot where Captain Cook drew his last breath of life.

Many years later, in 2010, I was in Edinburgh, Scotland, on my way to a legislative leaders' conference with our European counterparts. Being fascinated with Hawaiian history, Lydia and I took the long drive to Middleborough, England, to visit the Captain Cook Museum. Unfortunately, it was closed. The museum is on the edge of a field surrounded by a forest. Just off to the side of the building was an alluring tree. How can a tree be so enchanting? I don't know. I was drawn to the tree and walked the short distance to it. Under the tree was a water fountain and on it was a plaque. The plaque read that on this spot in 1728 Captain James Cook was born.

I realized at that moment that I'd had the unique experience of standing where one of the world's most renowned explorers drew his first breath in England—and that years before I had stood on the spot where he drew his last, on the shores of Kealakekua Bay.

2012

RANDOM THOUGHTS

RANDOM THOUGHTS and prose often pop into my head, often in the wee hours, and I've learned to write some of them down. Some of them may have been planted by other people—am I just subconsciously recalling them?

Summer Breeze
She slipped into the room like a soft wind that barely made the curtains move. Like an early summer breeze, she was warm, but not hot. She made it comfortable just being there.

Vulgar
It is easy to be vulgar; sadly nowadays some try hard at it.

Shadow
His shadow darkened the past; do not let it move over the threshold of the future.

Teacher
It seems odd that life's lessons creep up on you slowly, in such a way you don't realize you've been taught. That is what a good teacher does—teaches you life's lessons without letting you know. Lessons such as self-discipline, respect, honesty and even punctuality stay with you much longer than an obscure history lesson or algebra formula. Too bad so much has been lost in many contemporary classrooms.

Bell
Most ideas are like a bell that softly rings in a tranquil mind on the cusp of sleep.

Brightened by Darkness
Darkness makes light brighter.
Sadness accentuates happiness.
The storm is followed by tranquility.
Can we live in perpetual light, happiness and tranquility?

Why?
Much of America's contemporary pop culture and its media, certainly
television, music and print, have done an excellent job of finding vulgarity,
perversion and cruelty.

Sleep
He goes to bed at night not knowing how to fall asleep. After years of lazy
and easy sleep, slumber now seems to evade him. His mind is churning, his
thoughts are yearning, and then he sleeps.

Dogs
Dogs make you feel warm. They smell like dogs and that is good. Dogs
want to be with you and you with them. Their sometimes dolorous faces
are magically filled with happiness, especially for you. A bark can say so
much because you understand it better than words. Dogs are God's special
creatures.

About Riding Waves that Could Kill
Overcoming one's own fear is daunting, but the reward is nourishing and
broadens the horizons of life's experiences. Many of the great leaps of
humankind have been achieved by those who overcame fear.

Waves
The great waves of the surfing world die on the beaches of the island of
Oʻahu. They are born on the barren seas of the North Pacific and march
relentlessly to Hawaiʻi where, for a few fleeting moments, they unleash their
splendor and then disappear into memory. For an old surfer, such memories
are lifelong treasures.

Night Surfing

Please indulge me. We are faced with an ever more crowded world and more complicated challenges. Occasionally I like to make suggestions that may preempt problems and create more opportunity. Your feedback will be appreciated.

For instance, in the world of surfing many good waves are wasted. These are the waves that break in the dark of night. Taxpayers spend large amounts of money on land for recreational facilities with lights. Why not light up surf sites so surfers can ride the waves after dark? In Waikīkī, lighting the surf sites would not interfere with the nighttime optics of an already bright shoreline.

Of course such innovations always will be met with opposition, sometimes frivolous, but often loud and aggressive. Instead, I hope that true and bold civic leadership will find compromise and solutions. Think about it.

Ode to an Athlete Dying Young

I was never a literary intellect, but there is a poem that influenced my life. The poem is "Ode to an Athlete Dying Young," by A.E. Housman. A verse is as follows:

> Smart lad to slip betimes away
> From fields where glory does not stay
> And early though the laurel grows
> It withers quicker than the rose.

When the athlete died young, he never tasted defeat; he died a champion. I "retired" from competitive surfing after the 1968 World Championships. So it has been in my life. When I arrived where I wanted to be, I stopped my quest and pursued different challenges.

2015

THE PALI ROAD

I TRAVERSED THE PALI ROAD that clung to the cliff of the Koʻolau Mountains in the days of my youth. The road was closed in 1959 when the first Pali tunnel was opened. For the last decade I have lived in a home built next to my son and daughter-in-law's house on the old road. Their house is a sturdy home built of hearty timber. As in years gone by, the old house was built to last many generations, which it has. Heath and Daphne's house is the old Wong home, which was built in 1934. Wong was *consigliere* to the prodigious builder of Kailua, Harold Castle. Castle was a great surfer, too. I walk or drive my tractor on the old road regularly. It has been closed to traffic since the tunnels opened. I have even manicured a "park" on a sliver of land about one-fourth mile above our home. It is a park for children and dogs and those who love them.

I have read much about the related history of Nuʻuanu and the Pali. The first actual trail down the cliff was etched in 1845. The famous Mayor Johnny Wilson built the "modern" Pali Road in 1898. It served as the major road to the Windward Coast of Oʻahu until the Pali tunnels were completed in 1959. At the Pali Lookout there is a sweeping view of the Windward Coast. Often brisk trade winds are funneled through the Pali pass.

The old road included a well-known halfway house and store at the intersection of the road where the Kāneʻohe and Kailua legs separate. It is a site that dates back to antiquity. (For details, read the romantic tale in the book *Kaʻaʻawa*, written by O.A. Bushnell. All that remains of the old halfway house are the wide steps that now make up the trailhead for a wonderful hike to what I call "Fairy Tale Falls," a perfect little waterfall splashing into a tranquil pool carved into black lava.

During the Battle of Nuʻuanu in 1795, Kamehameha I and his soldiers fought their way up the valley to the lands of Laʻimi, where Laʻimi Road now lies just below Queen Emma's cool summer house. At that point Kalanikupule's troops made a stand at the Laʻimi Wall. Kamehameha had the support of his British advisors John Young and Isaac Davis, who helped him man several small cannons. When they fired at Kalanikapule's warriors, a shell hit the wall and its shrapnel killed the treasonous, heroic warrior Kai'ana. The disheartened warriors of Kalanikapule, upon the death of the seemingly invincible Kai'ana, retreated. Many O'ahu warriors and ali'i scampered up the sides of the valley. Those who fought to the death were pushed over a Pali cliff. You can, on certain nights, still sense their moaning spirits.

Kamehameha spent weeks rounding up the remaining O'ahu ali'i who escaped. They were clubbed to death at the *heiau* at Mount Lē'ahi and Papa'ena'ena and at a heiau in Moanalua Valley. Kamehameha the Great, as he would become known, was a ruthless warrior.

It always amazes me how history often is distorted to accommodate some other agenda.

2016
LOCAL BOY

HERE'S A STORY I WROTE in the genre of local humor, reflecting the Hawai'i in which I grew up. Much has changed in the Islands, but some things have not. Hawai'i's ethnic humor is funny, if not politically incorrect. Of course any resemblance to particular individuals is coincidental and not intentional. This story is rather involved for good reason. The ending is very complicated and, to better appreciate it, you need to understand the main characters—Masa, Moki and a gentleman of Portuguese ancestry, Manny.

So there are these three older local guys working construction in Kaka'ako. They're building a thirty-seven-story luxury high-rise on former Kamehameha Schools/Bishop Estate land. It will feature upscale condos listing from $1.6 to $20 million. Thanks to Sandra Day O'Connor and her U.S. Supreme Court colleagues, this is not leasehold land. Finally in Hawai'i, you actually can own what you buy!

The condo will be named Ming Tower after the Ming dynasty of China. In keeping with that theme the developer, Kukailimoku James, has appointed the Ming Tower with a Chinese decor. Even the elevator floors are numbered in regular numerals as well as in Chinese characters. The lobby will have an office for China Air, which flies nonstop from Beijing.

Smart? Wealthy Chinese are hiding their money in overseas investments. I guess they are smart Communists. It should be noted that locals can buy a condo, if they can afford it. Speaking of affordable housing, of course you all know compassionate Hawai'i has a law about affordable housing, but Mr. James is a big donor to the political process. Try wait. I am straying from the story. This is about Masa, Moki and Manuel, whom I am sure you want to meet.

Masa is the son of proud *nisei* parents Thelma and Daiichi Masanobu. Daiichi was a hero in Hawai'i's and our nation's most decorated and respected World War II fighting unit, the legendary 442nd Regiment. Many local boys have or had nicknames; even some of the haoles had nicknames.

(You may remember "Fuzzy" Castle, who played on the Punahou football team in 1964.) So Thelma and Daiichi's boy's nickname is Masa. Masa is happily married and a devoted father. He and his lovely wife live in Moʻiliʻili. Masa went to McKinley High School, did a stint in the Army and then became a skilled carpenter. He has been working for East West Construction for close to forty years. He always gets to the work site at 6:45 a.m. Masa is reliable and hardworking. In fact, he is the kind of guy who quietly builds Hawaiʻi.

Moki, on the other hand, is an outgoing, happy and contented Hawaiian. He is the son of Lehua and Brada Kekoa. Lehua and Brada grew up in Papakōlea. As Hawaiians, they both qualified to attend the fabulous Kamehameha Schools, but only Lehua was accepted for admittance. Lehua was so beautiful. She was a song leader on Kamehameha's cheering squad. Brada went to public schools. Though Brada can trace his lineage back to warriors, he and Lehua were old-style Hawaiians, full of aloha and not ʻaʻole.

Back to their son, Moki. Moki is a large boy and ended up playing on the Roosevelt High School football team as a lineman. It was the famous team that beat Kamehameha Schools on a rainy November night in 1964 and forced an Interscholastic League of Honolulu championship game. It was big stuff back then; 25,000 plus attended the Turkey Day game. After high school, Moki wanted to go to the University of Hawaiʻi and play football but ended up working at the Dole Pineapple Cannery in Iwilei. It closed when sugar and pineapple collapsed. Moki then took up construction and has been working for East West Construction for a number of years.

They say to save the best for the last. Manuel "Manny" Freitas Cunningham is half Caucasian and proudly half Portuguese. His great grandmother came to Hawaiʻi on the sailing ship *Hankow* from Funchal in the Portuguese archipelago of Madeira. It was 1883. I wonder if the Freitas heirs, as descendants of citizens of the Kingdom of Hawaiʻi, are entitled to reparations for the overthrow of their kingdom's monarch.

Like Masa's ancestors, the family of Manny's mother worked on the plantations. Miss Freitas attended Sacred Hearts Academy, a school for girls, which was almost mandatory for Portuguese girls from Kaimukī. She married Ted Cunningham right after high school. Ted was predominately of English and Irish ancestry. The family tree shows that a little French and Algonquin Indian crept into the bloodline. You know how those French guys are. So Ted went to Roosevelt High School and was proud that he and his classmate planted the big banyan tree in front of the newly built Roosevelt High School in, I think, 1933. That is all Manny heard about from his father every time they drove past Roosevelt.

To have a reasonable chance of going to heaven, Manny's mother insisted that he go to a Catholic school when he was young. His father had a burning desire to send all of his kids to Punahou. The Cunninghams were a family of modest means. Ted worked two jobs and Mrs. Cunningham took on part-time work. All their kids gained financial aid scholarships at Punahou. Manny worked in the cafeteria on scholarship duty. He played football. In fact, he was on the very team that won the legendary football championship game in 1964.

All the Cunningham kids surfed and paddled Hawaiian outrigger canoes. Manny was a pretty good surfer and the Cunningham kids were even on winning crews in the Moloka'i race. Manny married and has some kids.

So now the elderly Masa, Moki and Manny are in their waning years of employment. They are working on the twenty-ninth floor of the Ming Tower.

Toooooooot! The lunch horn sounds at precisely noon, as it does every day. Masa, Moki and Manny grab their lunches and sit down on the edge of the building. It is long way down. Their legs are dangling off the side of the building. Masa reaches into his *bento* box and pulls out two *inari* sushi. His eyes well up and he says loudly, "Inari sushi, inari sushi! That's all the missus packs in my bento every day. I tell you what, Moki and Manny, if I get inari sushi tomorrow, I goin' commit *harakiri*. I goin' swan dive off the side of this building."

Wow! Moki and Manny are taken aback by Masa's threat, so Moki reaches into his black lunch pail, takes out a thermos of ice water, and then pulls out a carefully wrapped *laulau*. He quickly explodes into a rage. "Laulau! Laulau this! Laulau that! I am sick and tired of laulau!" he says. "Masa, I goin' be just like you. If I get laulau for lunch tomorrow, I goin' jump off this building, too. That is it! I going *make*!"

Whoa! Manny is on the spot. He reaches into his paper bag where wrapped in waxed paper is a tuna sandwich on Love's white bread. Not to be outdone, Manny announces that he, too, is sick and tired of the same lunch every day. If he gets a tuna sandwich tomorrow he will do a swan dive off the side of Ming Tower.

So it nears noon the next day. Tooooooooot! The whistle heralds high noon and lunchtime. Masa, Moki and Manny grab their lunches and sit once again on the edge of the building. Masa reaches down and opens his bento. No inari sushi! His wife packed chicken *katsu*. Trembling, Moki opens his lunch pail and, lo and behold, no laulau! He has *pipikaula* and one *manapua*. Too good! All eyes fall on Manny. Manny reaches into his lunch bag and pulls out a tuna sandwich. In a fit, Manny stands up and launches off the side of the building.

Stunned, Masa and Moki look down on Manny's dead body. Masa looks at Moki and says, "I don't know what happened to Manny. He makes his own lunch."

Only in Hawai'i!

2016

MY LE JARDIN ACADEMY GRADUATION KEYNOTE SPEECH

Greetings parents, relatives, headmaster, teachers, staff and directors, and all the friends gathered here today at Le Jardin, and a special greeting to the honored graduates, the Class of 2016. Dear parents, it seems like yesterday that your daughters and sons were newborn infants. I am convinced that our Maker got it exactly right having babies born to the young. A newborn child is arduous work through night feedings and constant care. Those concerns are long since gone. Isn't it amazing how the toil of raising a child becomes a pleasant memory? Although your children are taking a large step out of your nest, they always will be your children. Surely, in the future, your adult children, with children of their own, your grandchildren, will come to you and say, "Hey, Dad. Hey, Mom," and a question or request will be asked. You will see not an adult standing in front of you, but rather your child. Although your offspring has grown up, he or she always will be your child.

Thank you, headmaster, teachers, staff and directors of Le Jardin. Stand tall; stand proud. Your labor and stewardship all these years has borne fruit. Teachers, it is obvious you are in the profession because of your desire to see this world become a better place; you have succeeded. I often reflect on why Le Jardin is such a special place. I think it is because you teach the kids and love them too. Pride in your accomplishments with Le Jardin's Class of 2016 should nourish you. A job well done!

Class of 2016, whether you have been at Le Jardin since preschool or started here more recently, you are and always will be part of the Le Jardin Family. Le Jardin has stimulated and enriched your intellect. You have acquired knowledge. The decisions you make for your own future will benefit from that knowledge. Your physical being has grown as well, strengthened through sports and the nourishment of your own body. You leave Le Jardin with strong minds and healthy bodies, but you have gained something in addition to knowledge and strength. You have learned something that has not been part of the formal curriculum. What you have learned may be the most important lesson for your future happiness. You have absorbed it and hopefully it is now part of your being: *virtue*.

Virtue is the essence of a better humanity. Human history remembers and honors most men and woman of virtue. Often virtue does not even have to be thought about. It comes to you naturally. Virtue comes from your soul. Virtue is recognizing goodness and striving for it, and yes, virtue is recognizing evil and standing resolute against it. Most of history is about that immortal battle.

Virtue is *tolerance*. How fortunate we are to have our differences, our individuality, our gender, our race, our religion; those differences are who we are. Certainly, we should not only tolerate those who are different from us; we should celebrate them. Our differences make the tapestry of life colorful and rich.

Virtue is *compassion*. Alexis de Tocqueville, a French aristocrat, in 1835 wrote *Democracy in America* and concluded, among many things, that part of the greatness of young America was compassion—that the best of America comes from our compassion for others. We as a society reach out voluntarily to help others, not because we have to, but because we want to.

Virtue is *gratitude* for your loving family, your teachers and all of those who have labored to bring you successfully to this occasion. Please, throughout your life, don't hesitate to express gratitude. Gratitude fuels goodness.

I pray that no matter what you choose for your future, you bring to your efforts, *passion*—that is, a burning desire in your heart to succeed. Believe in yourself and attack with passion all your future endeavors.

There are those among you who will have a passion for what is one of humanity's most curious traits—that is, a passion for the unknown—to reach out and touch what is not there, to go where no one has gone, or maybe to do what others have told you cannot be done. The greatness accomplished by humans is done by those who believed they "could." Those who thought they "could not" were probably right.

At no time in human history have horizons been so expansive. Some of you may have the passion to cross the threshold of safety and venture into the realm of risk, surely not because someone said you can't, but rather because you somehow know you can. A passion to succeed is what I call the Star Trek Gene, that is, to go where no one has gone. If you are going to take a risk, do so with the confidence to achieve your goals. Just think what thresholds you may cross. You may go on an interstellar journey to the cosmos, into a world that physics can't even explain. You may be the human being who finds a cure for a devastating disease.

Just a little more than sixty years ago, people were dying and lives were devastated by a disease called polio. A man named Dr. Salk changed all that. More than 100 years ago, Thomas Edison had a passion and failed many times before creating the electric light bulb; he never yielded.

You may choose a noble profession that makes the world a better place. You may be a teacher, those people who grow intellects, or a tradesman who designs and builds things to make others' lives comfortable.

Curiously, some of you will leave today not knowing what your life's passion will be. That's okay because time is on your side. The spark to kindle your life's passion will come to you.

The last virtue for your consideration is *love*. Love is the glue that holds humanity together. Love has and always will conquer hate and evil. Love will bring you ultimate happiness. Ask your parents about the love and pride you have kindled for them.

Let me close by paraphrasing a child's bedtime prayer heard in song years ago. For you, the Class of 2016:

> Bless you each day on the roads you go in all your
> tomorrows. May you sail to the far seas of fortune with stars
> to shine your way. There always will be angels to watch
> over you. May you bring love and may you bring happiness
> wherever you go. May you be loved in return for all your
> days.

Congratulations to the Class of 2016!

Family

2017

MY FAMILY

OF THE SIX HEMMINGS SIBLINGS, four are still pacing terra firma: Mark, seventy-six; Fred, seventy-one; Mia, sixty-nine; and Heidi, sixty-one.

We have traveled through time and space in my opinion in the most dynamic period of humanity. In our simple youth, space travel was fiction. Man now has walked on the moon and is making plans to inhabit Mars. We are observing the vast reaches of space. Talking and deductive machines were not even comprehended, information had to be researched in the *Encyclopedia Britannica* or in a library. Now almost all the world's information is on a smartphone in the palm of your hand. Most communication was by expensive long-distance phone calls that needed operator assistance; now a cell phone call is instant to the far reaches of the world. Medical science has leaped. Polio, which Mark, Mia and I had, and many other diseases have been eradicated. Titanium artificial joints keep us mobile, and hearts and organs are being replaced. DNA is unraveling the mysteries of our existence, and yet each profound advance opens doors to many more mysteries.

The phenomena continue at an escalating pace; singularity is on the horizon. What a time to be walking and living on this seemingly insignificant sphere in the infinite cosmos called Earth. Humanity has made this planet unique and profound.

Hawai'i is joyous. My siblings, wife, children and grandchildren give wondrous meaning to life.

2017

MY CHILDREN AND GRANDCHILDREN

I AM A LUCKY GUY!

I have four children and all of them are superstars.

My son, Heath Hemmings, is a very successful businessman. More importantly, however, he is a wonderful father of three children. He is married to Daphne Hemmings, MD.

My daughter, Kaui Hart Hemmings, is a renowned author and the mother of two. Kaui is perhaps best known for her novel, *The Descendants*, which was made into a motion picture starring George Clooney. Kaui is married to Andy Lautenbach, a prominent Honolulu attorney.

My daughter, Meaghan Hemmings, who lives in San Diego, California, is a financial planner. Her daughter, Kiera Leslie Lucero, is a super athlete at a young age.

My stepson, Gordon Kowalkowski, is on the superintendent's list and is a highly rated student at the Air Force Academy in Colorado Springs, Colorado.

With siblings Mark, Mia and Heidi, March 2017.

2011

A BEDTIME PRAYER FOR MY GRANDCHILDREN

Lay your head down, child of my child, and I will sing you a lullaby. May your sleep come to you with warmth and love.

Bless you each day on the roads you go in all your tomorrows. May you sail to the far seas of fortune with stars to shine your way.

There always will be angels to watch over you. May you bring love and may you bring happiness wherever you go. May you be loved in return for all your days. Now fall off to sleep.

Drift into the magic of a child's sleep knowing Papa loves you always.

(Inspired by some lyrics in "The Secret Garden" album.)

Dedicated to my grandchildren:

Trevor Ian Hemmings
Eleanor Hart Lautenbach
Eyosiyas "Leo" Andrew Lautenbach
Merrick Heath Hemmings
Kiera Leslie Lucero
Hanna Lillian Hemmings

Pau
I hope that when I die I am the person I want to be.

Index

About the Author

FRED HEMMINGS is a Hawaiian waterman, renowned outrigger canoe steersman and international surfing champion who won the World Surfing Championships in 1968. He retired from competitive surfing and inaugurated the world's first major professional surfing events, including the Pipe Masters. In 1976 he cofounded International Professional Surfing, the world's first pro surf tour. From 1984 to 1990, Fred was a Republican leader in the Hawai'i state House of Representatives. In 2000 he was elected to the state senate, where he served as a senate leader. A father and grandfather, he currently lives in Kailua, O'ahu, with his wife, Lydia, and his dogs.

Fred is a keynote speaker specializing in Hawai'i, surfing and tales of Duke Kahanamoku.

www.fredhemmings.com